CULTURE SMART!

CYPRUS

THE ESSENTIAL GUIDE TO
CUSTOMS & CULTURE

CONSTANTINE BUHAYER

KUPERARD

"The real voyage of discovery consists not in seeking new landscapes, but in having new eyes."

Adapted from Marcel Proust, *Remembrance of Things Past.*

ISBN 978 1 78702 260 7

British Library Cataloguing in Publication Data
A CIP catalogue entry for this book is available
from the British Library

First published in Great Britain
by Kuperard, an imprint of Bravo Ltd
59 Hutton Grove, London N12 8DS
Tel: +44 (0) 20 8446 2440
www.culturesmart.co.uk
Inquiries: publicity@kuperard.co.uk

Design Bobby Birchall
Printed in Turkey

The Culture Smart! series is continuing to expand.
All Culture Smart! guides are available as e-books, and many
as audio books. For further information and latest titles visit
www.culturesmart.co.uk

CONSTANTINE BUHAYER is a Londoner of Greek heritage. He has supervised for the International Liaison and Communication M.A. program at the University of Westminster, London, and lectured British military personnel, Chinese policemen (in preparation for the Beijing Olympic Games), and foreign journalists on culturally sensitive bilingual translation. He was also the country analyst on Cyprus, Greece, and North Macedonia for *Jane's Sentinel, Security Assessment*. He has reported on Greece and Europe for the BBC and Monocle Radio, and was guest Associate Producer on related CBS 60 Minutes programs.

Constantine was for many years a columnist on *Parikiaki*, a Cypriot newspaper in London, and a contributor to the Cypriot press. He has been active as an elected representative in political, community, and interfaith affairs in London, and is involved in Greek- and Turkish-Cypriot bicommunal dialogue. He is also the author of *Culture Smart! Greece*.

CONTENTS

MAP OF CYPRUS

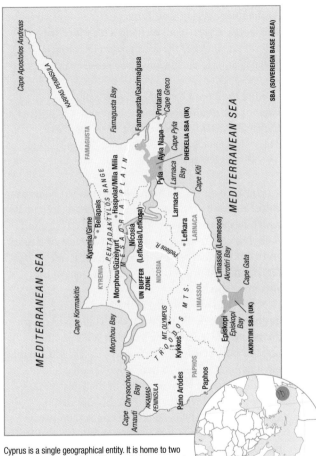

Cyprus is a single geographical entity. It is home to two political units. The Republic of Cyprus officially represents the whole island but does not control the northern section, which is occupied and recognized only by Turkey and is a *de facto* state.

INTRODUCTION

As shadows envelop your land
The winds, Cyprus, are blowing with your love.
You are the jewel of the Mediterranean, unique.
(From "Cyprus," by the Turkish-Cypriot poet Emine Otan.)

Land of the lemon tree, of the olive grove.
Land of the southerly winds.
Cyprus, this golden-green leaf cast in the ocean.
(From "Chrysoprasino Fyllo," by the Greek-Cypriot
poet Malenis Leonidas)*

As you fly over the Eastern Mediterranean, you see
glittering in the blue sea below the island of Cyprus,
which lies at the crossroads of Europe, Africa, and
Asia. Like Aphrodite, the Cypriot Goddess of Beauty
and Love, it emerged out of a primordial ocean; its
highest mountain, Troodos, is a fragment of that
ancient seabed.

More than any other sea, the Mediterranean
has been the crucible of great civilizations. Across
the island of Cyprus they have left not only their
imprint but their legacies down the ages, and current
ownership is subject to hard negotiations.

Indeed, history never stops. In the latest sequel,
the Republic of Cyprus was forcibly divided in
1974, its people dislocated. The Greek Cypriot
South is controlled by the government, attuned to
the world, a member of the European Union, and
accommodating the international community. All
this within a stone's throw from idyllic beaches and
the majestic landscapes of the hinterland. Visitors

will find a generous country enjoying a take-it-easy, *sigá-sigá*, *yavaş-yavaş* lifestyle, great food, and cultural heritage.

The breakaway North Cyprus is isolated but not forgotten. It is administered by the Turkish Cypriots and occupied and recognized only by Turkey, which acts both as its lifejacket and its Achilles heel. It contrasts with the South, but all communities on the island, even those who think they stand apart, possess a shared Cypriotness and common hopes and memories.

Culture Smart! Cyprus is unique in its approach. It combines essential insights into the Cypriot people of today—their values and attitudes, and the ways geography and history play into their lives—with practical advice on how to approach unexpected social situations, especially if on occasion you have the impression of walking on eggshells. What one person might see as cultural, another sees as political, and a third as territorial.

The Cypriots have a deep-seated experience of trauma and survival. They can present a variety of faces to confront, accommodate, or welcome outsiders as and when necessary. They are instinctively welcoming and generous and enjoy good companionship, lively debates, and mellow conversations.

So let the discovery begin of this multifaceted, surprising people, for the poet is right when she says Cyprus is "the jewel of the Mediterranean."

* Texts adapted from the Turkish and Greek by Constantine Buhayer.

Official Name	Cyprus or Republic of Cyprus (ROC). *Kypriaki Dimokratia* in Greek, *Kibris Cumhuriyeti* in Turkish
Flag	A white field showing a yellow silhouette of Cyprus above two olive branches. This is the official flag flying at the UN, the EU, etc. Designed in 1960 by the Turkish-Cypriot artist Ismet Güney, it has no "ethnic" color, that is, no blue or red.
National Anthem of the Greek-Cypriot Community	The Greek national anthem *Ode to Liberty*. There was no agreement on a Cypriot national anthem. This status quo is accepted by both communities.
Capital City	Nicosia. Lefkosia in Greek, Lefkoşa in Turkish
Main Cities	Nicosia, Limassol, Larnaca, Paphos
Area	About 3,571 sq. miles (9,251 sq. km), of which 2,276 sq. miles (5,896 sq. km) are under government control
Climate	Mediterranean, subtropical
Population	Estimated total: 1,215,826, of which 838,897 are in the official government-controlled territory
Currency	Euro
Ethnic Mix	Greek Cypriot
Family Size	2.3
Language	Official: Greek and Turkish. Armenian and Cypriot-Maronite Arabic also spoken.
Religion	Greek Orthodox. Some Muslims and Catholics
Government	Presidential republic with separation of powers between the executive and the legislature. The president is both head of state and head of government. Executive power is exercised by the government. Ministers are appointed by the president and cannot hold seats in the House of Representatives (Vouli Antiprosopon).

Government (contd.)	There are 80 parliamentary seats; provisionally only 56 are filled by Greek Cypriots. The remaining 24 are reserved for Turkish-Cypriot MPs when the island reunites. It has 6 MEPs (members of the European Parliament), including one Turkish Cypriot selected by the AKEL party.
Local Government Structure	There are six administrative districts covering the whole island as established since independence, and these officially include territory in the north, though government supervision is *de facto* excluded. Greek-Cypriot refugees from the north continue to hold official mayoral elections for their occupied towns.
Legal System	Mixed legal system, extensively codified but also heavily based on English common law. It is dominated increasingly by EU law. Judges are appointed by the Supreme Council of Judicature. The Supreme Court is the final court of appeal.
Cost of Living	The cost of living is cheaper than in Northern Europe, especially food.
Ports and Airports	Larnaca is the main airport. Paphos is a mainly tourist airport. Limassol is the principal passenger and cargo port.
Media	There are many radio stations and newspapers, including local English-language papers. RIK is the national broadcaster. Commercial and satellite stations are readily available. Several independent, often Net-based broadcasters
Electricity	240 volts, 50 Hz
Internet Domain	.cy
Telephone	The international code is + 357.
Time	Greenwich Mean Time + 2 hrs. Cyprus follows EU summer time.

Official Name	Recognized only by Turkey, the Turkish Republic of Northern Cyprus. *Kuzey Kıbrıs Türk Cumhuriyeti* in Turkish. Usually refers to itself as North Cyprus or TRNC.
Flag	Created in 1984, based on the official Turkish flag. A red star and crescent between two horizontal red bands against a white field. Recognized and used only by Northern Cyprus and Turkey.
National Anthem of the Turkish-Cypriot Community	The Turkish national anthem. There was no agreement for a Cypriot national anthem. This status quo is accepted by both communities.
Capital City	North Nicosia. Lefkoşa in Turkish
Main Cities	Nicosia, Kyrenia/Girne, Morphou/Güzelyurt, Famagusta/Gazimagusa
Area	1,295.4 sq. miles (3,355 sq. km)
Climate	Mediterranean, subtropical
Population	Estimated total, 326,000
Currency	Turkish lira. Euro widely used. No currency of its own
Ethnic Mix	Turkish Cypriots. Mainland Turks and Turkish Kurds now make up half the North's population.
Family Size	3
Language	Turkish
Religion	Muslim (Sunni). Greek Orthodox minority in Karpaz (Karpas Peninsula)
Government	A parliamentary republic with an enhanced presidency. A multiparty system where the president is head of state and the prime minister head of government. Executive power is exercised by the government. Legislative power is vested in both the government and the Assembly of the country.

Government (contd.)	Turkey plays a major role in its politics, which increases or diminishes depending on the ruling party in Nicosia. It has no MEPs.
Local Government Structure	It is divided into six districts, each with its own governor who has very limited powers. The enclaved Greek Cypriots in Rizocarpaso/Dipkarpaz elect their own *mukhtar* (leader) who has no legal personality in the North.
Legal System	"The judicial powers shall be exercised on behalf of the people of the Turkish Republic of Northern Cyprus by independent courts." TRNC Constitution
Cost of Living	Around 20–25% cheaper than in the South, but many goods lacking and the quality of some varies
Ports and Airports	Famagusta/Gazimagusa used to be the main port of Cyprus and is now a sleepy port. Kyrenia/Girne is the most popular tourist port. Ercan airport, due to the international embargo, only has flights to Turkey. The main airport of the North is now Larnaca International Airport in the South.
Media	There is a limited amount of media due to the small population size. Most Turkish-language output comes from Turkey. BRT is the state television, established in 1963.
Electricity	240 volts, 50 Hz
Internet Domain	.tr (the official domain of Turkey)
Telephone	+ 90 (the country calling code of Turkey)
Time	UTC + 2 hrs. Summer time is UCT + 3 hrs. This can change depending on whether it follows Turkey's time zone, which has changed back and forth over recent years.

CHAPTER ONE

LAND *&* PEOPLE

GEOGRAPHY

If in your childhood you played Cops and Robbers and used your hand to make the shape of a pistol, with this gesture you also made a handy map of the island of Cyprus, upon which you can locate its towns, regions, mountains, and beaches. For that matter, Cyprus' outline also looks a bit like that of the United States.

Cyprus is a European country with a global presence disproportionate to its size. Much larger than Hong Kong, Luxembourg, or Malta, and less than half the size of New Jersey or Wales, it lies on the quieter corner of one of the more earthquake-affected parts of the world and is subject to occasional shakes and tremors.

Its coastline offers no obvious natural harbors, mirroring the smooth coastlines of its Middle Eastern and Egyptian neighbors. The southern coast is interspersed with a scattering of difficult-to-access coves, a little to the chagrin of the tourist industry that pines for ever more brochure-style beaches, and which

The ruins of Buffavento Castle set into the steep, rugged crags of the Kyrenia Mountains.

successfully imported golden Egyptian sand to cover
stony strips. The duney north and east face no such
challenges.

There are two mountain ranges. The largest is the
vast complex of Mount Troodos, whose refreshing
valleys and escarpments finger their way down to the
dry coast in the south and to the outskirts of the wide
and at times dusty Mesaoria Plain in the northeast.
The second one is the narrow Kyrenia range, or
Pentadaktylos, running like a wall, parallel to the
northern coast.

Apart from the Pedieos River, the land is furrowed
by dry riverbeds, seasonal streams, and torrents that
can overflow in winter. The highest mountain is
Mount Olympus, at 6,404 feet (1,952 m).

Since Cyprus is an island that was never part of
a landmass, there was no movement of terrestrial
animals from distant places across its terrain. The

existing forms of wildlife were almost certainly imported by humans or arrived as stowaways and evolved there. This includes the long extinct and unique Cypriot pygmy hippopotamus, which shrank through a natural process. Today the island has a rich but fragile flora and fauna in need of fewer developers and more TLC. Worth pointing out in this land with a limited number of mammals are the unique Cyprus mouflon; the Cyprus mouse, with its Mickey Mouse ears, scuttling in the vineyards, which was recently recognized as a new species native to the island; and the Cyprus donkey, found in a feral state in the Karpas Peninsula and uniting Greek- and Turkish-Cypriot enthusiasts in ensuring its preservation.

The Black Whip Snake *Dolichophis jugularis* is the longest in Europe, reaching up to 9.8 feet (3 m). It is known as the gardener snake because it eats only rodents, insects, and other reptiles—just what the farmer wants.

Cyprus is a migration touchdown for millions of journeying birds. However, do say hello to the small disheveled, native Cyprus Warbler and the lithe Cyprus Wheatear if you come across them.

The native Cyprus Warbler overwinters in Israel, Jordan, and Egypt.

CLIMATE

The climate is semi-arid, Mediterranean. The reliably hot summers guarantee joyful holidays and busy air-conditioning units. Come winter, the weather is mild below the snow-capped upper Troodos range.

Water demand has now surpassed the supply from natural sources. The government in the South is building more salt-water desalination plants to achieve water self-sufficiency. In the North, Ankara partly controls this key resource, having built a pipeline under the Mediterranean providing potable and irrigation water from its southern coast to that of Northern Cyprus. Control of this flow is in its hands.

A HISTORY OF GIFTS, CONTINUITIES, AND RENEGOTIATIONS

Copper is the Name
The word "copper" comes from the name "Cyprus." In ancient times the island of Cyprus was copper rich, and sheets of processed copper were shipped far and wide. The Romans referred to it as *aes cyprium* (metal of Cyprus), which morphed into the word "copper." So any time you pick up small change, copper pots, or plumbing joints, in a sense you are picking up a bit of Cyprus history.

Ancient Times
Over the course of its long history Cyprus has interacted with Hittites, Achaeans, Minoans, Assyrians,

Ruins of the ancient city-state of Salamis, reputedly founded after the Trojan War.

Phoenicians, Achaemenid Persians, Eastern Romans/
Byzantines, Umayyads, Saracens, and Crusaders;
more recently with the Lusignan Franks and the
Venetians, the Turks, and the British.

The longest historical presence on the island
is that of the seafaring Greeks, dating back to the
Bronze Age. The oldest institution in its history,
one of the oldest in the world, is its Church, which
gained its autocephaly (independence) in 431 CE
at the Council of Ephesus; to this day its structures
influence social and political life. In fact, Christianity
arrived with the Apostles Saints Paul and Barnabas,
ensuring regular pilgrimages from far and wide.
Then, according to Acts 11:19, from this busy corner

Mosaic icon of the Virgin and Child at Kykkos Monastery.

of the Roman Empire, "men from Cyprus went to Antioch and began to speak to Greeks" about Christ. Today, the enduring Greek element makes the island the easternmost outpost of Europe, rather than the only Middle Eastern island.

As the Western Roman Empire crumbled, the Eastern Roman Empire (Byzantium) asserted itself on Cyprus for the next nine centuries. Saint Helena, the first-ever Christian Empress and mother of Constantine the Great, founder of Constantinople, spent time on the island. She offered it a fragment of the Holy Cross upon whose veneration she founded, around 327–329 CE, the monastery of Stavrovouni ("Mountain of the Cross"). It is one of the oldest monasteries in the world.

The House of Lusignan, or the Crusader Kings
In the buildup to the arrival of the Crusader kingdoms, Cyprus experienced drought, earthquakes, the plague

"The Queen's Window" in the upper ward of St. Hilarion Castle, with a sweeping view of the northern coast. Originally Byzantine, the castle was upgraded by the Lusignans.

The Gothic arches of Bellapais Abbey, founded by the Canons Regular of the Holy Sepulchre after the fall of Jerusalem to Saladin.

Painting of Guy de Lusignon from the Salles des Croisades at Versailles.

of 1174–75, and two eclipses of the sun.

The ruling house of Lusignan originated in Poitou in western France. In the late twelfth century, it sailed with the Crusades from a less developed Frankish Europe to conquer the more advanced biblical lands and Cyprus.

The Eastern Roman (Byzantine) kingdom of Cyprus had been quickly acquired by King Richard "*Coeur de Lion*" in 1192, who sold it to the religious military order of the Knights Templars. Within a year, it was handed to the Lusignans for their loss of the Crusader Kingdom of Jerusalem, and they remained overlords of this self-sufficient island for three centuries, until 1487. At times, the Mamelukes of Egypt and the Genoese held sway over a few towns or extracted their own income from the locals.

Immense business opportunities opened up when the Pope forbade trade with the "Infidels." This led to the city of Famagusta growing into a fabulously rich transshipment port. The arts flourished and there was a dazzle about the Lusignan court.

The Lusignans maintained a military administration that enforced a caste-like, feudal separation between themselves and the peasant-serfs (*parici*, in Greek). Furthermore, they were Roman Catholics who regarded the Greek Orthodox as schismatics—and vice versa. Most of the wealthy native Greeks suffered expropriation while the Frankish governing class was joined by Catalans, Italians, and other French. The division fostered native identity; for instance, the Stavrovouni Monastery remained under Greek Orthodox rather than Roman Catholic jurisdiction because the Cypriots bypassed the authority of the

Kolossi Castle outside Limassol was built by the Knights Hospitallers.

Catholic Church and negotiated directly with the
Lusignan authorities.

A few Greeks were emancipated by the Lusignans
from feudal slavery and could own land, the *lefteri*
(freemen). The seminal Cypriot chronicler Leontios
Machairas (1380–1450) was a French-speaking
Lusignan official who embodied a realistic respect
for papal authority with a conscious form of cultural
resistance. He famously authored *Recital Concerning
the Sweet Land of Cyprus* in an erudite form of his
native Cypriot Greek.

The most enduring legacy of the Lusignans is the
French Gothic structures and cathedrals, and the
sturdy, low-vaulted domestic buildings around the
island that stand as a unifying, national architecture.

Two Great Cypriot Queens

Helena Palaiologina was a Byzantine princess
who reintroduced Greek royal blood into Cyprus
through her marriage, in 1442, to King John II of
Cyprus and Armenia. She ordered her husband's
mistress' nose to be cut off, and went on to display
greater leadership than he did. She championed the
Orthodox faith and Greek culture by welcoming
educated Byzantines to the island both before and
after the fall of Constantinople in 1453. She died in
1458 at the age of thirty in the fortress of Nicosia.

Of all the crowns the Kingdom of Cyprus has
known, and it has known some, only Caterina
Cornaro reached "stardom." A wealthy Venetian
with sugar plantations on the island, she was its

last monarch (1474–89). She inspired an opera by Donizetti, which was revived in 1998, sponsored by Cypriot backers. It ends with Caterina promising her subjects no more unhappiness.

Caterina Cornaro, Queen of Cyprus, who was forced to abdicate by the Venertians.

The Venetians

The city-state of Venice had long been active on Cyprus through its merchants. They acquired it in 1489, but times were changing. In Shakespeare's *Othello* the eponymous hero is sent by Venice to defend it against "the Turk [who] with a most mighty preparation makes for Cyprus." The Venetians stripped the forests for the construction of ships and reinforced the existing fortifications against the new technology of the canon. Their strongholds still stand, including "Othello's Tower" in Famagusta.

In the arts, interaction with the Italian Renaissance under Lusignan and Venetian rule produced an Italo-Byzantine style that gave the two-dimensional Cypriot iconography depth and realistic rendering of the figures.

The Arrival of the Ottoman Turks

The military and diplomatic skills of the Turks had ensured their gradual conquest of the Levant. Now Cyprus stood as a challenging Christian island in an Ottoman sea.

In 1571, as the Turks were gearing up to annex the island to their empire, Catholic Europe reacted by sinking the Ottoman fleet in Lepanto, in one of the largest naval battles since antiquity. The French poet Pierre Ronsard wrote, "Preserve your beauty Cyprus from the Turk, embrace Mars, do not allow a barbarous Sovereign to take your island and tarnish your honor." On the ground, such idealism had limited appeal. Under their Venetian overlords the Cypriot serfs were confined to working the land, providing foot-soldiers, and supporting the court. They were open to a change. Ultimately the Turks rebuilt their navy, conquered the island, and sent over Anatolians, many of them with agricultural skills, to populate it with Muslims. They were Cyprus' first settled Muslim community and were joined by local, Greek-speaking Orthodox who converted to Islam to escape heavy taxation; they became an inseparable part of its composition.

By the early 1580s, a Cypriot in Tübingen told the Classicist Martin Crusius that the languages on his island were Greek, followed by Turkish, Armenian, Albanian, and Italian.

A stream of artists and intellectuals left for Italy, and especially Venice, to join a thriving Greek diaspora. With the control of the island secured, its strategic importance was neutralized. Neglect and restrictions turned it into a garrisoned backwater; a seventeenth-century Dutch traveler saw "canons lying about, dismantled and unused." Gothic cathedrals and many churches were turned into mosques by adding a minaret and eliminating figural representation. Artistic production continued, confined to ecclesiastical life.

Wealth lay with the Aghas, Ottoman officials holding the financial administration as tax collectors or tax farmers. Jealousy among them set off the first rebellion, around 1690, led by Mehmed Agha Boyajioglou. Constantinople had to send in troops that laid siege to Nicosia and Boyajioglou was executed.

The Present-day Impact of Ottoman Rule

The Ottoman *millet* system of administration evolved to give non-Turkish communities a level of autonomy within their ranks. For reasons going back to the Eastern Roman (Byzantine) Empire, the hierarchy of the *Rum* (Greek Orthodox) *millet* was Greek dominated. This ethno-religious separation led to a dramatic chain reaction. In the long run, the *millet* empowered the Church to become wealthy and a Greek national force in the nineteenth and twentieth centuries; it was used by the British to divide and rule; it determined the 1960 Constitution; and it shaped the partition of the island.

Orthodox religious leaders were elected by their community. Their position had to be confirmed by the Sultan, who did not grant any legal rights. He accorded them favors in the form of privileges that could be withdrawn at the stroke of a pen or with a beheading, most famously with the summary execution of the

Büyük Han ("the Great Inn"), the caravanserai in Nicosia built by the Ottomans in 1572 after their victory over the Venetians.

ethnomartyr Archbishop Kyprianos, during the Greek Independence War of 1821.

At grass roots level, the common experience of poverty and wretchedness had eroded the strict distinctions between Christians and Muslims. As a result, some Christians adopted, superficially and for practical reasons, Muslim worship. They were referred to as *Linobambaki* and survive to this day in the North.

The British Empire, or the Return of the West

In 1878 Britain acquired the lease to Cyprus from Ottoman Turkey. However, its strategic importance as a staging post to India evaporated after the British occupied Egypt with its superior port of Alexandria and the Suez Canal. Plans to improve the piers in Larnaca and Limassol were dropped and private investors found few attractions. While Britain exploited the island to the hilt by making the impoverished population pay for the lease, it did, however, replace the Ottoman system of favors and privileges with legal rights. Greek Cypriot notables began arguing for *Enosis* (union with Greece).

The First World War toppled empires and changed the balance of power on the island. Cyprus was still nominally Ottoman territory, and Turkish Cypriots identified as Ottoman Muslims—a badge that carried worldly prestige. But when in 1914 Turkey joined Germany against the Allied Powers, Britain retaliated by formally annexing Cyprus. After the war the Ottoman Empire was dismantled. Suddenly, Cyprus' Ottoman Muslims lost their "Motherland," and their elites felt a great sense of emptiness. Just as educated Greeks had left the island when the Ottomans took over in 1571, now many educated Cypriot Muslims left for mainland Turkey. One of those leaving was the first professional Cypriot photographer, Ahmet Sevki, whose portraits captured the faces of his fellow middle-class Turkish Cypriots. Turkish-Cypriot sociocultural life ground to a halt, and had to recreate itself. In 1923 Cyprus became a Crown Colony.

The 1930s saw widespread riots and strikes to improve worker's rights, followed by a liberalization of the regime and the official establishment of Communist-inspired parties. The rise of an industrial working class alongside the agricultural laborers meant the movements involved both communities. AKEL (The Progressive Party of Working People) began life in 1926 as the Communist Party of Cyprus, and won its first seats in 1943. The Turkish-Cypriot KATAK (Association of the Turkish Minority in the Island of Cyprus) was formed in 1943.

A WINDOW INTO COLONIAL CYPRUS

There is a mystery about the life of French *enfant terrible* Arthur Rimbaud. The little we know about his time in Cyprus is from his letters to his mother. After he gave up poetry, he sailed to Larnaca where new opportunities were arising from the British takeover in 1879. He found employment as a supervisor at an isolated stone quarry in Potamos Liopetrou, where he had to ask for a gun due to arguments with the workforce. Rimbaud wrote that it was a form of torture—dust, heat, fleas, mosquitoes, typhoid, and a European labor force constantly falling ill. Nothing but rocks, a river, and the sea. No trees, no gardens. The nearest village was one hour away by foot. Today, Liopetrou is strewn with bijou villas and swimming pools.

Then he became a foreman in the construction of the British governor's palace in the Troodos. Up there the British created a home from home, away from the heat and the locals. Wherever British garrisons expanded the Empire, they were followed by job seekers. That is how Rimbaud, and a host of Cypriot Greeks, left the island, taking their skills to deepest Egypt, Aden, and Abyssinia. They often acted as unsung pioneers of Empire, constructing encampments, establishing new trade patterns, and opening up previously inaccessible lands.

The Second World War

In the Second World War the population of Cyprus united against the Axis Powers, and soldiers of all communities rest together, for instance, at the Phaleron War Cemetery outside Athens. Some towns, such as Morphou, suffered aerial bombing and thousands of urban residents had to be evacuated to the countryside. Spitfire pilot and future president of Cyprus Glafkos Klerides became a hero of the Battle of Britain. Women broke away from traditional taboos and enrolled as nurses and took on jobs usually undertaken by men.

Independence, Not Union

In the 1950s, the movement for *Enosis* grew. The dynamic Greek-Cypriot leader Archbishop Makarios was a key supporter of a peaceful path to union. This, for the British, gave him a nuisance value equal to other anti-colonialists such as Gandhi, Nehru, Kenyatta, and Nasser. On April 1, 1955, the Greek-Cypriot paramilitary organization EOKA began a guerrilla war against the British, who responded militarily.

The Turkish Cypriots supported island independence, not union with Greece, so, with mainland Turkish training, they founded the paramilitary Turkish Resistance Organization (TMT). The Greek Cypriots were not against their Turkish-Cypriot compatriots, who formed 18 percent of the population. But soon intercommunal strife broke out—aggravated by the 1955 anti-Greek pogroms in Istanbul—risking a war between NATO allies Greece and Turkey, which would have weakened the Alliance

Archbishop Makarios on a visit to New York in 1962.

in the middle of the Cold War. There were also incidents of inter-Greek Cypriot and inter-Turkish Cypriot killings over the future of the island.

In 1960 Cyprus achieved independence, with political power shared between the two communities. Britain retained military bases in two Sovereign Base Areas (SBAs). Britain, Greece, and Turkey became guarantors of Cyprus under the Treaty of Guarantee.

The new president was Archbishop Makarios and the vice-president, Fazıl Küçük, who held the right to veto government decisions. He had secured constitutional safeguards for the Turkish Cypriots. He is revered in the North and respected in the South. In 1961 Cyprus joined the Commonwealth and refused to take sides in the Cold War, joining the Non-Aligned Movement.

By 1963 the constitution had proved unfit for purpose and intercommunal violence erupted. Around 20,000 Turkish Cypriots had to flee their villages into secure enclaves where they established their own armed and autonomous administration. To ensure peace, the United Nations Peacekeeping Force in Cyprus (UNFICYP) was established in 1964.

The Military Events of 1974

It was a hot summer's morning, July 15, 1974, and a perfect day for sharing out refreshing watermelons with home-made halloumi cheese. The holiday season was getting into its stride, with thousands of British and other European tourists enjoying the hot Cyprus sun. Suddenly, news broke on the radio that President Makarios had been killed in a coup; he survived, but the bubble had burst.

An extremist Greek-Cypriot coup was under way, led by mainland Greek Junta officers and with the involvement of the CIA. (President Clinton has since openly acknowledged the mistakes and horrors of official American support for the then Greek Junta and the Cyprus debacle.) The coup leaders aspired to unite the island with Greece, so they turned against the democratically elected government of President Makarios because, though he saw union as understandable, he was now adamantly against it, foreseeing it would lead to disaster. For the first five days it was Greek against Greek down the streets of Limassol, Nicosia, and across the fields. The Turkish Cypriots were initially safe; then they too came under wide and indiscriminate attack.

On July 20, Ankara invoked its right to intervene under the Treaty of Guarantee, claiming "to safeguard the independence, territorial integrity and security of the Republic of Cyprus." It launched Operation Attila with air attacks and troops landings in the north. This was also the first time in history that "an invading army had to contend with the presence in its path of a neutral third party in the form of an international peacekeeping force" (Brigadier Henn, at the time Chief of Staff of the

UN force in Cyprus). Then the Turkish army carried out its own massacres, with more than 1,600 Greek Cypriots disappearing (the *agnooúmeni*), and took over a third of the island, an act considered illegal by the UN. It also brought in tens of thousands of Anatolian Turkish settlers.

In 1983, against all international advice, Northern Cyprus' leadership unilaterally declared independence as the "Turkish Republic of Northern Cyprus" (TRNC), a move deemed unnecessary by many Turkish Cypriots. The UN called upon all members not to recognize the self-declared state, thus isolating the North from all international interaction, political, economic, cultural, and institutional. The outcome remains a near-total material dependence on Turkey.

At Last a Union, as in European Union

In 2003 the North opened checkpoints along the UN buffer zone (the Green Line), enabling cross-island movement for the first time in thirty years; this signaled a gradual relaxation of the border regime. In 2004 the UN's Annan Plan for the reunification of the island was put to a referendum. It had both flaws and advantages. Ankara and Athens, backed by the international community, encouraged the two sides to accept it. The Turkish Cypriots voted "yes"; Greek Cypriots said "no."

Within a week of the referendum Cyprus joined the EU, with the wider benefits of membership suspended for Northern Cyprus. In 2008, the island adopted the euro as its national currency. The Republic of Cyprus entered a major financial crisis in 2012–13 that saw thousands of households lose their hard-earned savings, and it suffered a major blow to its financial reputation. The EU and the banks were condemned for forcing the ordinary people to pay for a situation not of their making. The crisis also highlighted Europe's own trust deficit between its northern and southern states. But Cyprus soon recovered its reputation as an international investment gateway.

Manna from the "Mother Countries"

Despite some downturns, each Cypriot community has benefited incalculably from privileged access to the "mother countries" Greece or Turkey, to their markets, defense, and universities. Internationally, Nicosia availed itself extensively of Athens' diplomatic spadework, and Greek Cypriots traditionally achieve key positions in Greece. Meanwhile, Turkish and, especially, Greek companies profit Cyprus and themselves by relocating to the island.

But from the late 1990s Athens began to feel imposed upon by "needy" Cyprus distracting it from its own regional pursuits, not least rapprochement with Turkey. However, a hardening line from Ankara and its challenge to the Greek and Cypriot Exclusive Economic Zones, rebooted the Athens–Nicosia partnership.

THE GOVERNMENT

Traditionally the Republic of Cyprus is ruled by coalitions of center-right governments. On occasions the left-wing AKEL party has participated in the coalition; as a result social welfare remains an important factor in government policy. This has led to a social democratic, mixed-economy model. It even survived, slightly bruised, the 2013 financial collapse.

A JUDICIOUS APPROACH TO CHANGE

At first, the likelihood of Cyprus becoming an EU member state was a losing bet.

After the events of 1974, Cyprus risked turning into a non-destination. Then the collapse of the Soviet Union ended the Cold War and reduced its geostrategic importance. To boot, the Yugoslav succession wars of 1991–2001 were a warning against unresolved ethnic antagonisms. The bad news was that Europe did not want to embrace a new member at odds with itself. The good news was that European Union values promoted peace, security, and justice without internal borders, and that was going to be Nicosia's argument.

The new democratic government of Greece had promised Cyprus "what Nicosia decides, Athens supports." Nicosia wanted EU membership, therefore EU member state Greece kept its EU application on the agenda. In 1993 came the first official "Opinion" of the European Commission on Cyprus, describing it as "at the very fount of European culture and civilization."

Nicosia plowed ahead. For the first time in centuries, a new generation of Greek Cypriots was on a fast track, learning about international negotiation skills, finance, harmonization, and institutional changes.

Practical Faith

The popular wisdom of Nasreddin Hodja is valued across the East Mediterranean. One day, Hodja was singing on his donkey about the power of his faith. So a villager asked him to sing to the mountain in the far distance and make it come to him. Hodja tried, but the mountain stood still. Finally, Hodja headed for the mountain. "I am a humble man," he said, "and my faith is a practical one; if the mountain will not come to Hodja, then Hodja will go to the mountain."

A quick note on Northern Cyprus and the EU. Its leadership until the 2000s, dominated by then President Denktaş, opposed EU membership, arguing that it was *enosis*/union with Greece through the back door. But the electorate of Northern Cyprus went against this contention by voting "yes" for the Annan Plan, which included EU membership. Since then enthusiasm has waned, as demonstrated by the marginal victory in 2020 of a strongly EU skeptical leadership.

The grounds for a Cyprus solution envisage a bizonal, bicommunal federation. To many Greek Cypriots it sounds like a euphemism for segregation. To some Turkish Cypriots it doesn't go far enough in partitioning the island, which is what Turkish President Erdogan and a minority in the Turkish-Cypriot government started pushing for in 2021. But there are strong voices in Northern Cyprus that see partition as the undesirable final step before being annexed by Turkey.

NEWCOMERS FOR WHOM CYPRUS IS NO SURPRISE

Just a short 45-minute flight across the sea—about the time it takes to fly from Washington to New York—lies the Middle East. Cyprus, meaning the government-ruled South, has become an obvious neutral hub for all sorts of investments, where foreigners can enjoy a comfortable, high standard of living. There are more than 170,000 foreign nationals living and working in the South. A new foreign resident of Limassol from the region observed, "it is like home, without the unpleasant bits."

There are the Israelis popping in and out or living there, who see reflections of their own country with its ethnic and religious divisions, including a "wall," but with no apprehension of flying rockets. At airport arrivals, they stand relaxed with their Lebanese and Palestinian neighbors, waiting for their luggage. The business community over from Beirut is at home with intercommunal barricades and has twinges of regret over how once it was they who were the thriving, cosmopolitan business hub of the region.

The Chinese presence is expanding, especially around Paphos, where they are planning their own school. They are seen as very insular, especially since many do not even speak English. Meanwhile, rich Arabs settle into their own private luxuries. The Russians feel at home in a fellow Orthodox country with its abundance of churches and pilgrimages to take the family to, but with no strongman or harsh winters.

Numbering more than 20,000, they are reputed to be the highest per capita population outside Russia. Russian is the second-most important foreign language after English, featuring on financial brochures, church notices, tourist signs, and local wine bottles. There have been Lebanese and Jordanians settling since their troubles in the 1980s. The British form a large and established community of predominantly retired persons, comfortable with all the British quirks of the island. In the last ten to twenty years an increasing number of Americans have made Cyprus home.

Thousands of the new citizens—most of them respectable, some of them shady—have bought into the convenience of the country's "invest to obtain your permanent residence and Cyprus passport" scheme, which, more to the point, granted visa-free residency and working rights across the EU.

INVESTORS, ALLIES, AND SPIES

Foreign investors are sought, despite reservations being expressed that they are taking over.

And of course, there are spies. Who are the Americans seeing? What moves is the Russian Church making? How busy are the Greeks and the Israelis? What research is the UK High Commission funding? Are the Chinese bribing? Who is operating in the North?

The island has served as a convenient base for espionage since the Crusades. After the Ottomans the only spy in town was Britain, which erected giant radar intercepting domes on the Troodos. During the Covid pandemic lockdown, one of the rare jet trails in the emptied skies was Britain keeping up its strategic flights from RAF Brize Norton to its Cypriot base in Akrotiri.

The 1950s brought new intelligence personnel—Greeks, Turks, Arabs, Syrians, Egyptians. With the Cold War came the Americans who were anxious to keep tabs on the Soviet Russian interest, who themselves remain anxious to keep tabs on American movements, and on the Middle East. Now the French and Israelis want a share, and hold land, sea, and air training exercises with their Greek-Cypriot colleagues and hope to establish a naval presence: the former as part of a "*Grande Route de civilisation*" from Europe to India with an eye on francophone-friendly Lebanon; the latter to carry out security checks and give the green light to cargo ships heading to Gaza.

The US entertains the idea of having a Rapid Response Team, which the Republic of Cyprus classifies as being for "humanitarian operations." A useful word, "humanitarian," that bypasses Cypriot treaty obligations.

An unusual aspect of Cyprus as a "relaxation" destination was the Bloodhound Decompression Camp at Akrotiri SBA. British troops returning from Afghanistan and other war zones would land there to get help in working out their accumulated stress before continuing home. Even Prince Harry passed through on his return from serving for a few months in Afghanistan and enjoyed, as he put it, a bit of "blue sky."

NEWCOMERS TO THE NORTH

Northern Cyprus has different attractions and on a different scale; it is less developed, cheaper, quieter. The presence of the 30–40,000-strong Turkish military is ubiquitous. Brits and Europeans who retired to the North found this visibility uncomfortable. Eventually, it was decided that soldiers leaving their camps should wear civilian clothes. When you see groups of men who seem to have frequented the same tailor, the same barber, and trained in the same gym, they are probably in the army.

The latest influx of people is from African and Asian countries attending around twenty universities, including those with unaccredited programs. The students bring a youthful buzz to the North. But then the poorer international students need to earn their upkeep and some end up exploited in low-paid jobs, or worse. They number 15,000–20,000. Shanty town neighborhoods of migrant laborers have sprung up in some areas. Ultimately, most population numbers are speculative, not least those of foreign workers and the military.

CHAPTER TWO

VALUES & ATTITUDES

CYPRIOTNESS

What would Zeno, the third-century BCE philosopher from Kition (Larnaca) and founder of the Stoic school of philosophy, make of his island compatriots today? Perhaps that they live up to his recommendation, "We have two ears and one mouth, to listen more and talk less," but certainly that they understand the need to overcome adversity with equanimity.

The unresolved condition of the island is always at the back of their minds, creating a low rumble of existential apprehension; it is a way of life. A stoical Cypriot voice might well echo the sentiment in an article on the legacy of the Irish troubles in the *Irish Times,* "were we to tell our untold [Irish] stories, there would be no end of sorrow, living as we all did in varying degrees of extremity." Cypriots are a practical people; they still see fit to accommodate much of their difficult past by politely turning a blind eye to it and by raising a glass to the present.

Cypriot people can appear to be abrupt. Occasionally when encountering a Cypriot one may ask oneself, "He didn't say much, but is he being rude using that tone of voice?" The answer is no. For most, the boundaries between their agricultural roots and relatively newly acquired European decorousness are blurred. So, as in other parts of the world, any such abruptness is cultural, not personal.

If you think you understand Cyprus and the dance of its multiple identities, keep exploring and you will soon change your mind.

FAMILIES, RESPECT

Family is at the heart of society. Traditional family values embrace uncles, aunts, and first cousins. The young still respect the old in a wider sense; it is not unusual for them to address an elderly man or woman they don't know as "uncle" or "aunty" as a sign of respect." In this situation one also places oneself in the good graces of the older person. The endearing American "pops" or English "dear" do not express the level of respect of "uncle" or "aunty." On the other hand, obvious wealth and status in an older person seems to remove such a form of address.

A younger person in disagreement with their grandparents will tend to keep quiet rather than upset them. When a family attends a social event as a group, the members do not immediately disperse as if running away from each other.

In front of your elders, some formalities are adhered to. Ideally, because modern habits are kicking in, you do not chew gum, smoke, or consume takeouts in their presence. With your girlfriend or boyfriend you can be affectionate but not intimate. The tendency for young people to flick through their cell phones is seen as disrespectful. To disrespect your elders in public is tantamount to insulting those around them.

Entertaining guests in the West can be as informal as just having friends over. In Cyprus, from the moment of arrival, the formality of taking up a position to welcome you lasts a little longer. Upon arrival you shake hands with everybody present when introduced before being shown to your seat.

The exception to all this is children, who are free to run around. It's hard to imagine that they, too, will grow up in the footsteps of their parents.

Guests who are staying for two or three days are called *mousafiri*. If someone has *mousafiri* it means they'll be picked up at the airport if they are flying in, taken care of all day, shown about town, and driven to various sites.

COURTESIES

Thanking
In Cyprus thanks are used sparingly. There are contexts in which appreciative acknowledgment is implicit in the very fact that you have had a personal exchange. Not saying "thank you" is not a display of

indifference. "Thank you" is more common in formal situations. When someone offers water, a soft drink, or a house sweet, you can say "*náste kalá*," meaning "May you be well." But don't let that put you off from always saying "*efharistó*" in Greek or "*teşekkür ederim*" in Turkish. For greater emphasis in Greek, you can say "*sas efharistó*," the polite form of saying "I thank you."

To someone who holds a certain position in life, it is preferable to thank them warmly for *what* they have said or done rather than congratulate them on *how* well they have done it, because this implies that you also have the right to tell them they are wrong.

Congratulations

For Cypriots, the Western ease with congratulating seems over the top; it has little appeal—unless it is to do with family. Cypriots are accepting and relaxed but not overly effusive. Interestingly, they can begrudge what they see as other people's good fortune, so by praising one person you may find yourself disenchanting the person you are talking to. Saying "we met with so-and-so," is fine; adding "and we had a wonderful time, they are such good company," might be pushing it. In popular parlance a compliment is preceded by the Ottoman Arabic phrase "*Mashallah*" (literally, "God has willed it"). This is a way of expressing congratulations or appreciation with the inference that the ultimate author is good fortune or the grace of God, thus deflecting jealousy or averting the evil eye.

Major Requests
Preserving one's dignity and that of the other person
entails having the sensitivity not to openly put people
in a difficult position by requesting an important
favor or pushing them to acknowledge a mistake.
Major requests are best done through a neutral third
party to avoid the possible awkwardness of a refusal,
which can mark both parties. It is a culture where
interceding is readily available and woven into the
social fabric.

VILLAGE IDENTITY

To originate from the same village is tantamount to
belonging to the same clan. When applying for a job, a
person can be asked who their family is. The second-
best answer might include that one's father or mother
is from a particular village if it coincides with that of
the potential employer. The third layer is being from
Cyprus; an international Cypriot company in Athens
had an unspoken glass ceiling for mainland Greeks.

There is also a Cypriot look, or rather a range of
physical characteristics that identify people from
specific parts of the island.

As regards the two main ethnic communities, it is
often difficult to distinguish between them. According
to studies, the high percentage of thalassaemia
(an inherited blood disorder) across the Cypriot
population suggests "close contacts between the
two Cypriot communities during many centuries."

In effect, the physical similarities outnumber the differences.

THE VERBAL HIDE-AND-SEEK OF CYPRIOT IDENTITY

Citizens of Greece and Turkey tend to relate to the island of Cyprus as an integral part of their respective national and cultural narratives. An outsider who hears the words "Turk" or "Greek" will associate them with the two countries. In the mouths of Cypriots, these terms enjoy greater nuance according to the context in which they are used and whom they are addressing.

Now consider this. A group of Cypriots are talking, including Nikos who is a mainland Greek—you can tell he is an *Elladite* (mainland Greek) by his Athenian accent. At some point one Cypriot Greek will quip to Nikos that he is "a Greek," meaning he is not a Cypriot Greek and therefore cannot understand some things. Nikos can take umbrage and say "We are all Greeks," thereby prompting everyone to agree the obvious. Now you, an outsider, happen to join the conversation and you, too, hint at the differences between Cypriot Greeks and *Elladite* Greeks; it will not go down well because, irrespective of your intentions, your motives will be seen as suspect. Similar identity exchanges take place with Turkish Cypriots in the North. It is with some chagrin that a mainland Turkish bank manager, settled in the North with his family, observed that it is not unusual for a Turkish-Cypriot customer to remind him he is not from Cyprus. The situation is a little different with women because they are unlikely to do this to each other, but they can do it to men.

Given the art, literature, and history of Cyprus it is understandable that the Greek Orthodox of Cyprus once envisaged union with the rest of the Greek Orthodox, Greek-speaking world, rather than a separate island identity. It was also logical for the Muslims of Cyprus to engage with the Turkish world. However, there is undoubtedly a common, cultural Cypriotness. At a grand reception in New York one famous academic was talking in his native Greek, another in his native Turkish. So were they from Greece and Turkey? No. As soon as either of them spoke in English, you immediately noticed their Cypriot accent. The people of Cyprus keep alive, in varying degrees, their local (Greek *Kypriaká* or Turkish *Kibrislica*) dialects and a shared Cypriot accent, irrespective of the plethora of soap operas, game shows, or news programs they may watch on Greek or Turkish satellite TV.

From this one may gain the impression that one has to mind one's p's and q's when saying Cypriot, Greek, or Turk. That is not the case. It is fair to say that no offense will be taken; the longer-term resident might even learn to appreciate this native, verbal dance. One thing is certain: in business it is "Cyprus" and "Cypriot" all the way, and if negotiating in the north, "Northern or North Cyprus."

Don't Panic, it's Only PsyOps

A Greek-Cypriot doctor in Nicosia had developed inexplicable panic attacks. After seeing a psychologist, it emerged that his daily journey to his practice confronted him with the giant Turkish and Turkish-Cypriot flags in the distance, each 1,400 feet (430 meters) wide, painted on the southern slope of Mount Kyrenia in the Turkish-occupied North that overlooks the South. He changed his route and the panic attacks stopped.

The red of the Turkish flag has been allowed to fade but come nighttime both flags are ablaze with light. From her sunny office, an EU program coordinator also has a clear view of the flags. "You learn to ignore them", she says, adding that sometimes she imagines how if you removed the mountain, you would have a view of the sea behind it where her family used to swim.

THE PROUD PAST

Turkish Cypriots are brought up to take pride in the Ottoman conquest of Cyprus and of Constantinople. However, they also identify with the island's earlier history. They tend not to identify as descendants of Turkic nomads from Central Asia. Until recently the mother tongue of some Turkish Cypriots was actually

Cypriot Greek, because they were descendants of
Christian Orthodox converts to Islam.

Greek Cypriots are brought up to take pride in
their Ancient Greek civilization, if only because
their dialect has many direct similarities with
ancient Greek.

The ins and outs of allegiance frequently play out
in political campaigning. A leading Turkish-Cypriot
politician and supporter of "Cypriotism," said, "I feel
Turkish Cypriot. I cannot say I am only a Turk, only
a Cypriot. I am proud of both of them. They are the
cultural result of various historical developments.
The Cypriot side of my identity becomes more
powerful in reconciliation." Change "Turk" to
"Greek" and similar sentiments could be articulated
by a Greek Cypriot of similar political persuasion.

Turkey and Northern Cyprus do not recognize
the Republic of Cyprus, just *"Güney Kıbrıs Rum
Yönetimi"* or the "Greek Cypriot Administration
of Southern Cyprus."

At the end of the day, no Greek or Turkish
Cypriot will now deny, or joke about, each other's
Cypriotness, no matter how they understand it.

READING FLAGS AND MAPS

Official maps have a story to tell. Those printed by
the Republic of Cyprus represent the whole island
and all its features. The division lines are very thin,
thereby emphasizing Cyprus as a single unit without

boundaries. Across the northern area of the map, printed in light lettering, is the label "Area Under Turkish Military Occupation Since 1974." The place names follow modern English usage. The maps of Cyprus do not show all the roads of the North because sections of them may have been built over Greek-Cypriot owned land.

North Cyprus maps present their territory as a separate country so they often show only the northern part of the island. The original Turkish place names are kept but the Greek names are changed into new Turkish ones.

Today, both sides can cross the Green Line. The North is open to shoppers from the South for its fresh groceries, cheaper gasoline, made-to-measure bedding items, and imitation labels. The South is open to fellow Cypriots from the North as commuter workers and to shop. Above all, there are new initiatives, a new generation that can mobilize—and fewer chaperones. A new common culture is being added to the existing one.

DIVIDED NICOSIA: A PSYCHOLOGY OF CYPRUS

Among all cities, Nicosia stands out as the last capital in the world whose fortifications still function as defenses. It is also the last divided capital. Some of its cultural monuments come under the supervision of the Department of Arts and Culture, while others come within the strategic purview of the Ministry of Defense or of the UN's Peace Keeping Force.

A short stroll brings into focus instructive juxtapositions. As you cross Zaha Hadid's ultramodern Eleftheria Square, which hugs a section of restored fifteenth-century Venetian wall, walk round the tennis courts beneath the Tripoli bastion that today encloses a dull parking lot and you arrive at Paphos Gate. Here things get serious. It is topped by the white and blue defensive oil drums of a Greek police station and a bunker. The Venetian wall morphs into a militarized border with Turkish north Nicosia but with kids playing ball beneath Mula Bastion. Eventually you arrive near Ledra Palace, once a luxury hotel, then UN HQ, and for decades the only venue on Cypriot soil for bicommunal discussions. The old city wall then dozes off as it continues its circle into Turkish north Nicosia, a little crumbly where it survives, before reaching a barricade and back into Greek south Nicosia and the tourist illuminations of Famagusta Gate.

From Paphos Gate the actual border line turns right, cutting the old town in half and enclosing a UN guarded, ghost-city within two cities. This is not Venetian, but a DIY wall left by fighting factions from 1963, consisting of a succession of bricked-up houses, oil drums, and sandbags blocking the narrow streets. On the Greek side these installations have looked so temporary for so long. On the Turkish side the wall is concrete and looks like a permanent military border.

Are Differences Cultural or Political?

I was fortunate to be the only observer allowed
at a week-long symposium held behind closed
doors for young Cypriot professionals from
both communities. This was the first encounter
between groups of young professionals from each
community since partition (and before the Green
Line had opened up). Events were structured
to initiate intercommunal engagement and the
sharing of experiences and aspirations. In the
debates, the Turkish Cypriots were reserved
and initially contributed only if invited by the
chairman. The Greek Cypriots were spontaneous
and expressed diverging opinions; later some
thought they were "freer" to do so. When one
official speaker asked for a show of hands on the
possibility of EU membership "as though the
problem on the island did not exist," the majority
thought he was being naive. During lunch break, I
engaged freely on a one-to-one basis with Turkish
Cypriots who expressed various views. When I
engaged with them as a group, I was met with a
polite, collective silence and they deferred to one
person who seemed to express the official line.

Above the city, in the quiet of the night, a
household projects a Charlie Chaplin film onto the
building across the narrow street. On the ground,
Greeks and Turks, students and tourists, cross the
Green Line to shop, work, party, and unite for joint

cultural projects. Below, the sewage system of both sides enjoys a bicommunal wastewater treatment plant. There has never been a sewage war.

A STRONG DIASPORA OF VILLAGES

In Britain, especially London, there are more than 200,000 Greek Cypriots and over 70,000 Turkish Cypriots. As British subjects, they began arriving in the 1950s, escaping dire agricultural poverty and later the conflict. Since the 1990s they have migrated as skilled professionals.

As they settled, Greek Cypriots established local Greek Orthodox churches, then opened Greek Saturday schools for their children. Most parishes function as Cypriot villages that run their own earthly affairs. For the older women, many of whom kickstarted their diaspora families by working as seamstresses, the church is a second home in a changing world.

The old country matters dearly. The Limassol-born British Cypriot magnate Theo Paphitis stated that "in the Diaspora, Cyprus has a second Cyprus abroad." His friend, Famagusta-born Touker Suleiman, entrepreneur and fellow TV personality, is keenly attached to his Cypriot roots. Stelios Haji-Ioannou, whose Easy Jet low-cost airline revolutionized air travel, keeps returning. So many became high achievers that they featured in a special publication of "Greek Rich List." Singer-songwriter

George Michael (Giorgos Panayiotou) in his soulful song "Round Here" evokes his Greek-Cypriot father disembarking in London, "My daddy got here on the gravy train . . . it was 1957 and love felt the same." Some British Cypriots, like the artist Tracey Emin, of Turkish-Cypriot heritage, know their "ancestral connections go back a long way," but with the death of loved ones back on the island they "feel Cyprus slipping away" from them. Others consolidate the attachment by buying property there.

Doing the Right Thing

The Eastern Orthodox faith in Britain would hardly register if it were not for the large presence of dynamic Greek-Cypriot communities. The Greek-Orthodox Diaspora comes under the ecclesiastic jurisdiction of the Archbishopric of Thyateira and Great Britain, part of the ancient, Istanbul-based Ecumenical Patriarchate of Constantinople. Relations are civil, though when "Constantinople" is perceived to support the Turkish government in areas inimical to Cypriot concerns, it damages relations with its Cypriot members in the UK and in America, and angers the government in Nicosia. In a recent move, some British Cypriots have argued for an autonomous British-Cypriot Orthodox Church with Cyprus actively at its heart.

A Lively Media

The British Greek-Cypriot community pioneered in late 1989 and 1990 the first foreign-language services to be granted broadcasting licenses in Britain. They are London Greek Radio (LGR) and Hellenic TV, now reaching a worldwide Greek-speaking audience.

Another organizing factor of the community in the diaspora is the British branch of the AKEL party. It advocates "Cypriotism," that Greek and Turkish Cypriots share the same aspirations and cultural identity. It publishes the oldest British Cypriot newspaper, *Parikiaki* ("of the community"). Poignantly, its weekly obituaries over the decades constitute a history in faces. The center-right newspaper *Eleftheria* is rich in historical articles. The Turkish-Cypriot newspapers include *Londra Gazete* and the monthly magazine *North Cyprus*, featuring local personalities, recipes, and life back in Cyprus. All the papers have English sections and online editions.

Diaspora Impact on Cyprus

During the decades when the border between North and South was sealed, things moved on in Britain. There, Greek and Turkish Cypriots continued old village friendships. The older generation lobbied parliament. The younger generation held joint groundbreaking conferences and Cypriot arts festivals; they campaigned united for political office and against racism. At least three British Foreign Secretaries have highlighted this harmony as an example to follow. When the border in Cyprus opened, those skills were picked up by locals from both sides.

WOMEN CHANGING PLACES

Women in the Republic of Cyprus experience to a large extent the same privileges and obstacles as those in much of the European Union, whose Directives provide standards for women's rights.

Cypriot women in employment are more frequently represented in lower-paid occupations and with pay equality lagging behind, even if on average they have a higher level of education than employed men. Considering that until the 1960s many were illiterate or went to school for just a few years, things are obviously improving. Slowly, the state is addressing the gender pension gap that can leave older women at risk of poverty.

On corporate boards, the representation of women is low but increasing due to EU efforts to impose female quotas. There is a low proportion of women in politics.

However, when social customs kick in, the picture changes. Traditionally men and women saw the home as the realm of the wife. As such, it is accepted for Cypriot men to find food ready on the table and the house looked after. Today, most women in towns work and face the fact that they cannot do everything, irrespective of house pride. Of course, children will eventually look after their parents if necessary. New lifestyles mean that a number of these duties are today passed on to domestic helpers, with Filipinos as a first choice, and then other Asians.

Women in towns are found working in the public sector, the family business, at councils. In the villages they stay at home more and share work in the fields.

In the North, there is no EU to motivate changes, and fewer jobs to foster a wider sense of independence. There is no flirting as such with Western outsiders. It is expected that if a Christian, meaning Greek, woman marries a Muslim, she will take on his religious affiliation. The strong secular values of the country mean that younger Turkish-Cypriot women can now stand up for themselves to a degree.

GAY RIGHTS

Same-sex partnerships have been gaining acceptance in Cyprus since it joined the EU. The adoption of the English-language term "*gey*" (gay) accommodates local conservative sensitivities; it normalizes "gayness" albeit by hinting that it is a Western choice. LGBTQ persons are not usually open about their lifestyle, but hatred based on sexual orientation is a criminal offence. Homosexuality was decriminalized in 1853 by the Ottomans, though a stigma lingered in public perceptions. It was recriminalized under British law in 1929, and finally legalized by the Republic of Cyprus in 1998, and by Northern Cyprus in 2014.

NOSTALGIAS AND COMMONALITIES

Cypriots do flag their roots. The most poignant nostalgia is how well integrated they used to be. Many a modern poem by local *poitáres* is infused with memories of past joys, including the food of ordinary people, bread, sardines, smoked herring, olives, halva, and also with current affairs. A famous poem about Cyprus by Turkish-Cypriot Nese Yasin, "Which Half?" was set to music by Greek-Cypriot composer Marios Tokas.

Poetry is key in Cypriot culture. At an official level, it has celebrated mainland Greek or Turkish cultural allegiances, but not only. For independent Turkish-Cypriot poets it is a way of exploring a collective Cypriot memory down the ages, and their poetry is also relished by Greek-Cypriot activists and academics.

CYPRIOT VIEWS OF THE OUTSIDE WORLD

Perceptions of the outside world in the Republic of Cyprus have undergone a sea-change. Its new international initiatives to attract foreign investors bring into focus China, India, the Gulf States. Its security needs, too, include new partnerships, Egypt, Israel, Jordan. They supplement its love–mistrust relationship with the USA and the UK. This is all quite fresh and is being slowly digested by the Cypriot media. The older perceptions remain, justifiably holding outsiders responsible for its division, but also relying on them as distractions from its own responsibilities.

A PYLA OF HOPE

Pyla is the only village in Cyprus where the original two communities live side-by-side, a microcosm of the island between 1963 and 1974. It lies entirely within the UN buffer zone. The affairs of Pyla are regulated by the UN. The Greek and Turkish communities live alongside each other but separately, with their own schools, their own flag poles, their separate Greek and Turkish coffee houses and tavernas. Any dispute is tackled by the UN guardhouse. The village is famous for offering most things illegal with minimal interference. Behind the closed doors of so-called Internet cafés lies a not very salubrious world. However, sit at the central taverna unaware of its status, and things seem peaceful to the point of boredom, except for the Turkish army observation post perched on a hilltop above, overlooking the old Venetian watchtower restored with EU funds. Since 2012, Pyla has hosted the state-of-the-art overseas campus of the British University of Central Lancashire. Head further 15 miles (25 km) east and you are at the world-class, coastal resort of Ayia Napa.

The Republic of Cyprus maintains 43 embassies and high commissions and 124 consulates. The most important locations are Washington, New York, London, Brussels (the EU), Moscow, and Athens. These cities also have Cypriot correspondents, while most foreign news reporting relies on foreign news agencies. Invariably the outside world is gauged by its willingness to support Nicosia's effort toward a "just Cyprus solution."

Northern Cyprus has one embassy, in Ankara, and representative offices in 24 countries. It appears its staff do not have diplomatic visas.

The Church of Cyprus has ancient links to the Orthodox authorities in Lebanon, Jordan, Jerusalem, and Alexandria, having provided them with priests, bishops, Patriarchs, as well training clergy. It has a representation to the EU in Brussels.

ATTITUDES TOWARD FOREIGNERS

The sharp increase in the number of foreigners settling on this bustling, thriving island has created cultural contiguity and a cosmopolitan, albeit cautious, buzz. Local attitudes toward them vary. How far should they open up their economy without losing control? Some warn, "We are opening traps and we don't know how to close them."

Domestic workers are mostly women from Asia, who at times almost become "family." But their rights are on hold because the "frozen conflict" tops civil society priorities and the political agenda. Bulgarian and Romanian migrants, as Eastern Orthodox, can be integrated under the wider Greek umbrella (as per Article 1 of the Constitution). High-income foreign professionals are welcome; many reside around Limassol, earning it the sobriquet "Little Texas."

Many immigrants from developing countries have crossed illegally to the Greek-Cypriot South from Turkey via Northern Cyprus, compounding local concerns of being overwhelmed. There is a perception that criminality is high in areas they frequent; however, as meaningful contacts increase such attitudes shift, especially toward genuine refugees whose plight the Cypriots recognize.

There are more than 50,000, mostly retired, house-owning British people living in South Cyprus. They are organized and unobtrusive. Regarding those living in Northern Cyprus, an older British couple residing there described in a good-humored way some of their peers as "looking like extras out of the film *Hatton Gardens Job*," about a real-life London heist. The younger generation of Brits is more outgoing and networked. In both parts of the island they enjoy sound relations.

Regarding property, "anyone with documents relating to the purchase of property in the north of Cyprus when crossing the Green Line could face criminal proceedings" in the South.

CHAPTER THREE

CUSTOMS & TRADITIONS

THE PAST IS CONSTITUTIONAL

As we have seen, for historic reasons religion in Cyprus determines which community and sub-community you belong to. Articles 1 and 2 of the 1960 Constitution state, "the Greek Community comprises all citizens of the Republic... who are members of the Greek-Orthodox Church. [...] The Turkish Community comprises all citizens of the Republic... who are Moslems." The same Constitution adds extra ethnic and linguistic criteria. Furthermore, for those Cypriots outside these two groups, Article 3 determined that they could choose once and for all to opt to belong to either the Greek or the Turkish community. There was no option for "just Cypriot." These other communities are the Armenians, the Maronites, and the Latins. Though small in number, they are equally native and chose to be "Greek" and are all represented in parliament. But there is more to it than that, as may become clear below under the heading "Other Religions."

THE CHURCH OF CYPRUS

Greek Cypriots have strong religious convictions but there is no proselytizing, or even any discussion of their faith.

When the Saints . . .

The religious calendar provides the annual rhythm of life in the Republic of Cyprus, not just with the major Orthodox Christian festivals but with its numerous saints' days. This means it's *panegyri* time in towns, villages, and monasteries to celebrate, on the allotted date, their own patron saint. The occasion is a compound of festival, feast, and fête, organized especially during the warmer months. The feast

Scene at the *panegyri* of the hillside village of Amargeti, to the east of Paphos.

At the heart of the community: the church in the mountain village
of Moutoullas in Nicosia District.

starts in the morning at the local church; then people gather outside where communal chairs and tables have been laid to indulge in food, music, local wines, and dancing. There are stalls selling homemade Cypriot specialties and handicrafts. Later in the day people sit together, order more substantial food, talk, and relax. It can go on into the early hours of the morning, uniting all ages from all walks of life, bringing together people who have not seen each other since last year.

Influence
The election of the Archbishop of the Orthodox Church of Cyprus is a nationwide process that stirs spiritual, political, and geopolitical debates and embraces the clergy and congregations of every local church. Overall, the Church influences but does not determine social and political life. Besides, in true Greek fashion, there is a lively polyphony of voices and debates among the clergy. The Church of Cyprus runs its own TV channel and newspaper.

Cypriot churches are also meeting places; together with the monasteries they owe their wealth to their investments and the donations of the faithful.

Etiquette
Church etiquette is standard. If you enter a place of worship, make sure you are not wearing "nice little nothings" as James Bond would put it, especially in monasteries where dress code observers are vigilant. Arms and legs should be covered. A coin or two in the donation box is welcome, but a must if lighting a candle.

If you decide to sit, under no circumstances cross your legs or put your arm around your partner—it is not a taverna. During liturgy you may hear a whispering chitter-chatter from the faithful in the pews, which stops at especially holy liturgical passages or at the invocation of the *"Panagia,"* the Holy Virgin. It is standard for parishioners to kiss or air kiss the hand of the priest when receiving a blessing.

Icons

Ecclesiastical art can be so refined as to feature on UNESCO's World Heritage List. However, icons are venerated regardless of artistic merit, and some are considered miraculous. According to St. John of Damascus, "the invisible things of God since the creation of the world are made visible through images." To reject icons is to reject the humanity of Christ; their presence inside the church counts as the physical presence of the *Panagia*, Christ, and the saints standing among the faithful.

Churches also stand as points of

Icon of Agios Stylianos (Stylianos the hermit), patron saint of children and orphans.

geographic reference in giving directions. People will explain that they live in sight of a specific church, or a ten-minute walk or drive from it.

PRIESTHOOD

The practicalities of the priesthood are exemplified at the Theological Seminary of Apostle Barnabas in Nicosia. It also has Eastern Orthodox students from the Middle East, Africa, Greece, and beyond. In order to be accepted as a student, free of charge, a future priest needs the blessing, meaning the approval and recommendation, of his local bishop. Though the courses and liturgical life are intensive, students can obtain breaks to follow key sporting events outside the premises, since there is no television. The future priest can have a full family life but must marry before his ordination, which must take place with the written permission of his wife. If he is married, he will not be eligible to rise in the ranks. His wife will be addressed as *presbytera;* she does not have to follow his regime but needs to be faithful, kind-hearted, and modest in her appearance, which does not mean plain or boring. Many priests' wives have jobs of their own or run a family business and choose to be active in the life of their husband's parish.

RELIGIOUS BUILDINGS IN THE NORTH AND SOUTH

In parts of Cyprus, along the Green Line, one can sometimes hear the ringing of church bells alongside the call of the *muezzin* to prayer. There are still a few functioning mosques in the South to accommodate the spiritual needs of the Muslim immigrant workforce and refugees from Syria and Asia. The most famous mosque complex on the island is the modest but iconic Hala Sultan Tekke, with its profile reflected in the Larnaka Salt Lake beside it. It contains the tomb of Umm Haram, the foster sister of Prophet Mohammed's mother and wife of Ubadah ibn al-Samit, one of the companions of the Prophet. It is considered the third or fourth holiest place in Islam after Mecca, Medina, and Jerusalem.

The Hala Sultan Tekke mosque on the serene shores of Larnaca Salt Lake.

Orthodox churches in the North are in a sorry state. Some have been looted, defaced, used as agricultural or army depots, or been bricked up to prevent further destruction. No one should try to visit them without permission, even if there is a washed-out sign outside stating they are a museum. There is no animosity toward churches, but the Turkish-Cypriot authorities have no emotional reason to maintain what many had seen as symbols of oppression in the 1950s and '60s. On the other hand, the authorities restrict Greek Orthodox services. An exception is made for the miracle-rich Monastery of the Apostle Andrew (Andreas) at the emblematic tip of the island, Cape Apostolos Andreas, or Zafer Burnu, on the Karpas Peninsula. A steady stream of pilgrims and regular filled-to-capacity services ensure its condition is not deteriorating. Some explain that the site with its saint was also honored by Muslim pilgrims and hence has not been closed off.

ISLAM, SECULAR MUSLIMS, AND RELIGION IN THE NORTH

For centuries and at a local level Cypriot Islam offered an accommodating, integrated way of life of coexistence. As pointed out above, to be a Turk was to be a Muslim; there was no ethnicity attached to it. In the Republic of Cyprus Constitution of 1960 Cypriot Turkishness is defined as a people whose "mother tongue is Turkish or who share the Turkish cultural traditions, or who are Moslems."

The annual calendar adheres to the main religious holidays. Lately the fast of Ramadan is more widely observed, following the global trend in Muslim communities. Out of politeness, visitors may refrain from eating, drinking, or smoking in public during Ramadan.

The mosque is the main space where the imam leads prayers and teaches the word of the Koran. You can enter a mosque, but not during a service. Take off your footwear where indicated at the entrance. Women should cover their heads and exposed flesh.

Turkish Cypriots are Sunni Muslims, but mostly in a cultural sense, and they object to Islamic fervor being imposed on them; consequently they can be resented by some Muslims, not least by those Turks who pursue an all-embracing form of Islam.

The massive, newly built Hala Sultan Mosque outside Nicosia in Haspolat (originally Mia Milia in Greek), funded by Ankara by the government of President Erdogan, has a capacity of 3,000. Its Ottoman–Byzantine rhythm echoes the great mosques that embellish the Istanbul skyline, and it dominates the Mesaoria Plain for miles around. Overall, in its scale and mission, it is removed from the secular spirit of Atatürk and does not embody the social values and historic evolution of Turkish-Cypriot identity.

CYPRIOT AND TURKISH TURKISHNESS

There are an estimated 160,000 "immigrants from Turkey" in Northern Cyprus, mostly rural Turkish

settlers with some Kurds brought over after 1974, but also Turkish military and their families. Mainland Turks who moved there independently include educated, liberal individuals who love the lifestyle. The rural settlers are quite distinct. Many were used to eating sitting on the floor; their formal education lagged far behind that of Turkish Cypriots, while their social values and regional Turkish dialects marked them out as separate. However, mixed marriages tend to enhance "Cypriotness." Those who have been granted North-Cypriot citizenship can vote in the North, though unlike Turkish Cypriots they cannot enter the Greek-Cypriot South.

However, there is a dearth of reports on the new communities of the North, and how they affect Turkish Cypriots and the future of the entire island. Officially, the Constitutions of Turkey and the TRNC proclaim membership of the "eternal" and "inseparable" Turkish Nation. But so many modern-day Turkish Cypriots, like

Turkish-Cypriot participants at an international folklore festival in Skopje.

Leontios Machairas before them, remain adept at the art of cultural resistance, sustaining through lifestyle, negotiations, respect, and poetry their native Cypriot character.

OTHER RELIGIONS

Members of the Armenian, Roman Catholic, Maronite, and Latin Church minorities chose in 1960 to register with the Greek community, which was defined constitutionally by its religion. They enjoy rights regarding personal status and statutory representation in a number of Cypriot institutions.

The Armenian community has a long presence in Cyprus and was boosted in numbers after the 1915 Armenian genocide. Numbering only around 3,500, they are Greek speakers but also have their own language, schools, and churches and play a significant role across the Armenian diaspora.

The Maronite community currently numbers fewer than 6,000 souls. Many arrived on the island centuries ago as Christian refugees from Syria and Lebanon. They speak their own dialect of Cypriot-Maronite Arabic, or Sanna, with numerous Greek loan words, though none have declared it as their first language in the South. Their villages were in northwestern Cyprus near Cape Kormakitis, and most fled to the South following the Turkish invasion. Those who remained are now elderly, speak Sanna, and are allowed to work their land.

The Latin community is basically Roman Catholic and traditionally skilled, sophisticated, and urban, with roots in the Venetian centuries of the island and joined by French, Ragusans (from Dubrovnik), Italians, and Maltese. The community is growing and slowly morphing through intermarriage with Catholic migrants from Europe, but also now from the Far East. It receives state assistance for its schools and churches, and free health care for Roman Catholic clergy irrespective of their nationality.

HOLIDAYS TO REMEMBER

The main public holidays in the South are readily available on annual calendars.

January 1 New Year
January 6 Epiphany
February (movable feast) First Lent Sunday followed by Clean Monday
March 25 Greek Independence Day and Annunciation Day
April 1 Cyprus National Day
April, early May Good Friday (half day), Good Saturday, Easter Sunday, Easter Monday
May 1 Labor Day, Spring festival
August 15 Feast of the Assumption of the Virgin
October 1 Independence Day
Ochi (**"No"**) **Day** 28 October
December 25 Christmas Day
December 27 St. Stephen's Day

THE IMPORTANCE OF SAINTS' DAYS

The Greek Orthodox invariably choose a name for their children that is also that of a saint, most often that of a grandparent or a loved family member. You may almost certainly forget a birthday but if you know the name then you know the name-day, especially since everyone around you will, from friends and family to coreligionists, to virtual friends on social media. Guests drop round to offer their good wishes, or send them by e-mail or on social platforms, and wish them many years, or *hrónia pollá*. It is a great opportunity to renew contact, maybe to initiate a healing process if any misunderstanding has occurred in the past.

The most popular names are:
January 1 Vasileios, Vasilis, Vasiliki
January 7 Ioannis, Ioanna, Yannis, Yanna
January 17 Antonios, Andonis, Antonia
February 10 Charalambos, Harris
March 25 Maria, Marios, Evangelos, Evi,
    Evangelia, Vangelis
April 23 Georgios, Yorgos, Georgia
May 5 Eirini, Irene
May 21 Constantinos, Kostas, Eleni
June 29 Petros, Pavlos (Peter, Paul)
July 7 Kyriaki, Kyriakos
July 17 Marina, Marinos
July 28 Chrysovalantis, Chrysovalentina, Afxentios,
July 20 Ilias (Elias)

August 15 Maria, Mary, Marios, Panagiotis,
Panagiota, Pezoula, Despina
October 6 Thomas
October 26 Dimitris, Dimitra
November 8 Michalis, Angelos, Angeliki
November 25 Aikaterini, Katerina
November 30 Andreas, Androula
December 6 Nikolaos, Nikos, Nikki
December 9 Anna
December 12 Spiros
December 27 Stefanos, Stephania

THE GREEK-CYPRIOT YEAR

January 1, New Year or *Protohronia*

This is Saint Basil's Day. All households and most
businesses, organizations, and sports clubs cut
the *vassilópita* (special new year cake). Everyone
receives a slice. The person who finds the coin
hidden within will have a lucky year. The *vassilópita*
ceremony can take place any time in January for
non-family organizations.

January 6, Epiphany

This is the Blessing of the Waters and celebrates
Christ's baptism. Priests bless the waters (sea, lake,
or river) by throwing in a cross. Young divers jump
into the water and the one who retrieves and lifts
it is blessed for the year.

Party time at the Limassol Carnival.

February (movable feast), Carnival

The carnival climaxes a week before the Lenten fast of *Megali Sarakostí*.

March 25, Greek Independence Day, Annunciation of the Virgin

Shared with Greece. This anniversary celebrates the day the Greek flag of independence was raised against the Ottoman overlords at the monastery of Hagia Lavra in Greece. It is also a religious festival.

April 1, National Day of Cyprus

This marks the start of the 1955 independence struggle.

April to early May, Holy Week and Easter Sunday

The Greek Orthodox faith is centered on the Resurrection, known as *Pascha* or *Lambri*. This by far is the most important festival in its calendar. Throughout Holy Week, starting on Palm Sunday, beautiful liturgies are held following the stages of Christ's Passion. On Saturday at midnight the light of the Resurrection is lit. On Easter Sunday Lent fasting ends with a tremendous feast of roast lamb and everyone cracks dyed red eggs.

May 1, Labor Day

Demonstrations take place asserting workers' rights.

August 15, Assumption of the Virgin

A very important festival in the middle of the holiday season when families travel from far and wide to get together.

October 28, *Ochi* Day

Shared with Greece. This marks the time when the Greeks refused to surrender to the Axis Powers and fought back victoriously in 1940 and early 1941.

December 25, Christmas

The Christmas Day mass is particularly beautiful.

High school students participating in a solemn parade on *Ochi* Day.

THE TURKISH-CYPRIOT SECULAR CALENDAR

1 January, New Year's Day, or _Yılbaşı_

23 April, National Sovereignty and Children's Day
Shared with Turkey, this day commemorates the opening of the Grand National Assembly of Turkey at Ankara in 1920 during Turkey's War of Independence, which saw the Turkish Republic emerge as the last state out of the Ottoman Empire.

1 May, Labor Day

19 May, Commemoration of Atatürk, Youth and Sports Day
Shared with Turkey, this commemorates the start of the liberation movement that Atatürk initiated in 1919 when he landed in Samsun on the Black Sea.

20 July, Peace and Freedom Day
Anniversary of the start of Turkey's 1974 Operation Attila in northern Cyprus.

1 August, Social Resistance Day
Anniversary of the founding in 1958 of the Turkish Resistance Organization, or TMT, in opposition to the Greek-Cypriot EOKA.

30 August, Victory Day
Shared with Turkey, this commemorates the 1922
victory following the Turkish War of Independence
that removed foreign powers from its soil.

28–29 October, Republic Day of Turkey
Shared with Turkey, this is the day the Republic of
Turkey was founded.

15 November, Republic Day of TRNC
This day commemorates the 1983 Declaration of
Independence.

MUSLIM FESTIVALS

These religious festivals follow the Muslim lunar
calendar and so the dates are movable.

Eid al-Fitr
This is a three-day celebration marking the end of the
month-long fast of Ramadan. It is a time for sweets to
be shared around, for giving presents to the children,
and sharing food.

Eid al-Adha
This is the most important religious festival of the
year, lasting four days. It commemorates the story of
Abraham offering his ultimate submission to Allah by
accepting the command to sacrifice his son Ishmael.

Lambs are "sacrificed," albeit by professionals, for celebratory meals.

Ramadan

The holy month of Ramadan involves a regime of fasting between the rising and the setting of the sun, when the faithful abstain from food, drink, smoking, and sex.

The Prophet's Birthday

This is a day for reading devotional poetry and celebrating the name of the Prophet. In recent years it has seen organized pilgrimages from the North to the Hala Sultan Tekke mosque in the South.

RELIGIOUS HARMONY

The faith leaderships of Cyprus have received much praise for their cooperation in taking significant steps toward religious freedom, human rights, peace, and reconciliation. In 2021 the Archbishop of the Greek Orthodox Church of Cyprus, Chrysostomos II, warmly thanked the retiring Mufti of Cyprus, Dr. Talip Atalay, for his tireless work and for being the first Mufti in Cypriot history to engage in dialogue with the leaders of all the island's faith communities. Chrysostomos' words were echoed by the local Armenian, Maronite, and Latin Catholic religious leaders.

that are formed during youth are loosened after marriage. Then the wider family comes into sharp focus, with its plethora of family occasions.

Some such occasions are open to friendly outsiders who attend as guests, such as baptism and marriage where your presence is an honor. Special venues are hired out for weddings, because they tend to be large, huge, or immense. Invitations are distributed personally by hand—it's quite a marathon. Some weddings attract thousands of people who will be offered nibbles and a drink. The full three-course wedding meal extends only to several hundred. To accept the full invite implies you will be handing over a *fakeláki,* an envelope with money, and it really will be noticed and circulated if you don't make the gesture. The presenter of an empty *fakelaki* will be found out. However, during the famous Cypriot wedding money dance, as an outsider you are not expected to pin layers of bank notes on the bride's flowing white wedding gown as it turns orange and green from the colors of the 50 and 100 euro banknotes pinned on it by friends and family. Baptisms are treated like small weddings, though the only pinning will be done by the godparents—of the *filaktó,* a thumb-size pouch containing holy relics.

More private though not exclusive occasions are funerals if you have a connection with the deceased, but also memorial services if you get to hear of them. These take place in a church forty days after the death and then annually. More exclusive events are the welcoming parties for family members who are leaving or especially returning from a long stay abroad. Birthdays are events where close friends can be expected to turn up, and name days are inescapable since to know a person's name is to know their *yiorti*. The custom is for a party to be thrown on the person's name day. A barbecue and buffet at the house are prepared, and there is lots of singing, dancing, and drinking. Invitations are not generally given to join the celebrations of a name day—friends, family, and neighbors drop round. As you meet more people, you'll be surprised at how many share the same name and surname, though this does not necessarily mean they are related.

The shift from rural to urban life on the island has impacted upon the nature of friendship. Cities are synonymous with apartment dwellings and therefore routine encounters with neighbors are less frequent and it is more difficult to meet up without having to spend money on entertaining. Belts were tightened during the 2013 financial crisis when the banks in Cyprus were briefly closed. People woke up to see their savings lost, gone, and found themselves living on a fifty-euro a day subsidy. This was a shock to the system and to social life on the island. Though the closure lifted, it left scars and a note of caution.

HOW TO MEET CYPRIOTS

"I do entreat that we may sup together.
You are welcome, sir, to Cyprus."
(Othello, in Shakespeare's *Othello*)

Outdoor café in the wine-producing village of Omodos, Limassol District.

It is socially relatively easy to meet people in Cyprus since you will often bump into each other—nowhere is too big to disappear. If you intend living there, albeit for a short while, it pays to interact with people, and you will not find yourself ignored or isolated. The challenge, or the comfort, with the recent establishment of communities from other parts of the world is that you can gravitate toward your own people, so to speak, especially if they host social events through clubs or activity groups.

Cyprus is a café society and there are plenty of occasions when people will talk to strangers. Choose your regular café and you will soon be absorbed into the banter of the fifty or a hundred regulars. If you are upset by something, you change coffee shops. There is also your regular swimming beach, should you prefer one. There again you can soon make lovely acquaintances. These places offer a friendly forum for practical or philosophical queries about life in Cyprus. Not least, you, too, may be able to help others based on your own experiences.

Drop By, Tune In

So now, how much do you want to get into the Cyprus rhythm of life? Cypriots are careful with strangers to the point of appearing hesitant, even toward Greeks in the South and Turks in the North. They are quite reserved and can be clannish. They can seem moody to someone used to the merry banter and openness of Greece and Italy, or the seriousness of Turkey. Upon meeting, in the spirit of *philoxenía* (affectionate love for the stranger) they will warm to your presence and the interest you show, only to follow this the next time by displaying a more formal attitude. This is not personal—it's about confidence-building steps. It is best not to fire questions at them, though exchanging family information is welcome. Because Cypriots can make loyal friends, you will in time be able to explore the meaning of Cypriotness as your presence becomes seamless.

A good place to meet people, if you are invited, is at a *soúvla*, or barbecue, in someone's garden. Holding a *soúvla* is both an important event and very gregarious and comfortable to attend. If you are lucky and have access to an open space, you too may wish to hold a *soúvla*, be it for three or four people as a starter; make sure there is more than enough food and drink for everyone—good BBQ skills can earn you plaudits.

On the other hand, if you are on the island with the mindset of a long-term tourist, you have the pick of cosmopolitan tourist beaches.

A regular place for bumping into friends and colleagues is during the *vólta*, the promenade. This is the leisurely stroll around the village square, but especially along the sea. It is one of the quietest and most relaxing activities as families or groups of friends amble in the cooling late afternoon or refreshing evening, stopping for an ice cream or to greet someone. To join a friend in this activity is to have face-to-face contact with a wide range of people.

If you feel the need to complain while shooting the breeze, make sure it is not about local issues, unless it applies to your tribulations with bureaucracy.

INVITATIONS HOME

If invited to someone's home, it is customary to take a gift. In the afternoon, a box of traditional Cypriot or Western-style cakes from a *zaharoplastío*, or patisserie, are in order. In the evening bring wine or cakes, but not flowers—a potted plant is fine if the household appreciates them. Flowers, half-joked one

Cypriot friend, cannot be eaten. They can be offered to women on their name day, or else something small like an icon, which is also good for men, or a book. It is rude not to do so. Gifts must always be wrapped—don't turn up with a naked bottle in hand. Shops have pleasing bags and an array of glossy paper to choose from and will gift-wrap your present beautifully, even the box of patisseries. You might be asked if it's for you or a present and there is no extra charge. When handing over your gift, do it quietly.

Whether you are hosting or are invited, bear in mind that guests may bring a friend; it is not considered gate-crashing. If you want to bring a friend to someone's home, just call beforehand to confirm with your hosts. When a new member of the family or a new guest enters the room it is standard to stand up to greet them, or to be introduced to them. If it is the first time you meet someone, say "*hárika*," meaning "It gives me joy."

With presents such as a scarf or an item of clothing, it is good to provide an exchange card in case they wish to change it; after all, you are not expected to know their size or their color preference.

Two local expressions characterize hospitality in Cyprus—"good heart" and "the table always laid," meaning there is always food on the table for people dropping by. Across Cyprus a guest is well fed and their plate is filled when emptied. There are no small portions, calorie counters, or empty stomachs. Be ready to hit the gym or swim extra lengths the following day.

NAMES AND VERBAL GREETINGS

In Greek there is the polite form and the informal
form of address, exactly like the French *vous* and *tu*.
A simple example is saying "hello." The polite form is
yiá sas, the informal from is *yiá sou*. The polite form
is used for people older than yourself, strangers, and
individuals in positions of authority. It is rude not
to do so. It also applies when addressing someone
you don't know and until you get to know each other
better, when you may be invited to speak in the *enikós*,
the informal form of address. If in the slightest doubt,
stick to the polite form.

When meeting someone you have encountered
before, with whom you've exchanged personal
information, it is acceptable to ask how the family are
and to observe that the children must have grown.
One can also ask for one's greetings or respects to be
passed on to the whole family if you have met them.

If you are meeting someone on their name-day or
birthday it is very good to greet them directly with
"*hrónia pollá*," meaning "May you live long."

When walking into a restaurant it helps to say hello
in the local language, "*hérete*" in Greek, or "*merhaba*"
in Turkish.

In the South, people shake hands and give a small
smile. In the North, the same act is accompanied
with a modest inclination of the head, an echo from
the days when people bowed. A nonverbal form of
greeting between good friends in the South is kissing
or air kissing twice on the cheeks, even with a friend's

wife or husband, followed by "How are you?" or "How is the family?"

ACCEPTABLE CONDUCT

To grow older is to command greater respect, in both communities. There is no rushing older persons and to show what might be perceived as impatience is to disrespect the whole family.

If someone is speaking it is considered impolite to interrupt them, as is asking pointed questions or openly challenging something they said.

There are trigger topics that are best avoided. Best to put off talking about the North and South and the Cyprus problem. In the South, the North is regularly referred to as *katehómena*, meaning occupied lands. In the North, references stress that the South is Greek and therefore something of a separate entity, and criticizing anything about Turkey is usually a no-go area unless you have local experience and hear Turkish Cypriots being critical. Criticizing aspects of Greece in the south is acceptable so long as it is not overdone, especially as Greece is also a fellow EU state and, in some respects, a competing state in tourism and shipping.

If someone has suffered the loss of a close one or a colleague, it may surprise you how controlled, almost sphinx-like, they may seem about the sad event, almost north European. It is good to offer your condolences and leave it at that. Cypriots have learned to bottle up a lot of things.

Respect People's Sensitivities

One thing to remember is that idle talk about
the Cyprus problem can hurt and alienate people
for whom the trauma of the conflict has left a
lasting sense of betrayal. Here is a very likely
scenario; a Greek- or Turkish-Cypriot friend or
acquaintance tells you an interesting story about
their visit to the North or the South, or about
friends in the other community. You may wish to
mention what you've heard to a different group
of people, in your own words, through your own
understanding. Refrain from doing this, and
certainly don't mention people's names. As your
acquaintance with the country deepens, you may
reach a point where you think you understand
the factors at play. At such a moment remember
the words of David Hannay, the former British
Special Representative for Cyprus, that "like
Sisyphus" he pushed up the hill the stone of
understanding the sensitivities at play, "only to
see it roll back again several times." He eventually
retired to receive a life peerage and write a book
about those experiences.

TIMEKEEPING

People can be an acceptable ten to twenty minutes
late. Then there is the excusable "Nicosia traffic" late,
of up to one hour. Traffic there can be horrendous.

If you are on a home visit, then the time to leave is before siesta time in the afternoon, though enquire if this applies as the custom is being relaxed due to Westernization. In the evening, leave before midnight.

WHO PAYS?

The person who initiates the invitation is usually expected to pay. If you suggest going out for a meal and your guest jumps in to pay the bill, you can remind them how you wanted to invite them; but often he will respond that you are a guest in the country and that *philoxenía* means they will pay. This applies to the first, possibly the second, time. Then it will be up to you to return the compliment. If a large group of you go out, then sharing the bill equally is usual.

In a group of four or five, it is not unusual for someone to take the initiative and pick up the tab and for someone else to challenge him; and it is a "him," for it is usually between men and it is a question of pride. Cypriots are practical and down-to-earth. Those who have more money may well wish to pay, even for a large group, and there will be no obligation to return the gesture. To ask for the bill, catch the waiter's attention by raising your hand and scribbling in the air.

Cyprus coffee served the traditional way.

ALCOHOL, COFFEE, AND POLITICS

I drink therefore I am political—well, almost. To drink KEO beer can still indicate that you support the left-wing parties, while Carlsberg beer shows an alignment with the right-wing parties DISY and DIKO. Likewise for coffee. Laiko coffee—meaning

People's Coffee—is associated with a left-wing clientele, Haralambous coffee with a right-wing clientele. They are both rather good. The proliferation of alcoholic products and types of coffee from around the world has diluted these allegiances but they still tend to apply in some social clubs frequented by older citizens. There are no prizes for guessing what is consumed in the offices of the very powerful left-wing PEO union or in those of the right-wing SEK.

A must-try-several-times drink is the typically Cypriot liqueur Zivania, similar to the Italian *grappa* or the French *marc* and produced exclusively from the first distillation of wine, grapes, and pomace. Its alcohol per volume is up to 60 percent and it is best consumed accompanied by Cypriot appetizers. On a good night or hot summer's afternoon a bottle or so will keep the company going and the stream of appetizers make as good a meal as any. Aged Zivania is much prized.

Cypriots do not get drunk in public, which is frowned upon; they do it in private. The legal blood tolerance concentration (BAC) in Cyprus is zero, perhaps with good reason—driving standards are among the poorest in Europe. If someone has had one too many on a night out, their drunken demeanor is absorbed by the overall bonhomie of his group. Cheers! *Yámas!* *Şerefe!*

Zivania is appreciated around the island. As for the opaque and delicious local coffee, should you say Turkish coffee or Greek coffee? It is "Cyprus coffee,"

North and South, and its original recipe goes back
centuries when it was brewed in Damascus with added
cardamom pods. Coffee is offered when making a visit
or meeting someone at an office, and the length of its
consumption can be a civilized way of measuring the
length of your stay—neither too long for your host nor
too short for yourself.

ROMANCE AND THE FOREIGNER

Not so long ago Cypriot couples dated with a view to
getting married. Usually they had been introduced
by *broxeniá*, match-making by family friends or
relatives. Today individuals make their own choices,
with *broxeniá* only occasionally invoked. According
to experts on dating in Cyprus, the difficulty for
interested parties is crossing that "do I dare?" moment.
Cypriot men, they say, tend to think of Cypriot
women as being "little princesses" and difficult to
approach, while the women think Cypriot men are
unforthcoming. Words to describe potential wooers
include: shy, reserved, even "What will the parents
think?" Admittedly, "one-night stands" have always
taken place on the island, from the days when Cypriots
worked in the fields to playing the field in today's
clubs. A foreigner should remember that people
in Cyprus tend to approach dating as a means of
getting to know the other person, and then we'll see.
Invariably, the man pays when going out. Cypriot
women who are more relaxed about dating tend to

have a marriage behind them and a sense of personal independence.

Cypriot women who marry foreigners tend to choose Greek Orthodox men from Greece, sometimes from Lebanon. Men marrying out will be a bit more international.

In the North of the island, cultural Islam is not that strict, the dress code is Western, and views vary on whether things are more difficult or easier than in the South.

For any visitor just wanting a summer romance, the isle of Aphrodite is rich in like-minded holidaymakers worshiping sun, sea, and sand.

TRANSACTIONAL SEX

Light years away from the felicities of romance is the so-called oldest profession. Prostitution, as in the selling and buying of sex on a one-to-one and consensual basis, is not illegal in the South. HIV testing is only voluntary, however, and the results are officially confidential; venereal clinics are readily available. Today, in the South, brothels and organized prostitution are not legal but there are still places where sex is bought indirectly through the purchase of a drink. In the North things are worse (see page 155).

CHAPTER FIVE

AT HOME

"Cypriots build houses as though they'll live for ever and eat as though there's no tomorrow," goes the Cypriot saying, meaning they build solid, luxurious homes. The eating part speaks for itself.

HOUSING CHOICES

There's also a new Cypriot saying, "Give people money and they will start competing," referring particularly to Cypriots among themselves. Competition involves ostentation.

Modest Cypriots like a house with a small garden or a courtyard. Whenever they can, they'd rather purchase the land and build a house, generally through a contractor. The philosophy is: clear the land, build, and don't look too closely at planning regulations. Integrating construction with the natural environment is not a priority. Sometimes the result is pleasing.

And another saying, "How do you know that the daughter of the house is now independent from her parents? They have built a house for her above their own." Certainly, for family reasons, new houses like the option of an extra floor or two.

The obsession—and it has to do with a misplaced sense of prestige—many have in Cyprus, and across the wider region for that matter, is for a lush, green lawn, just like those in damp and rainy northern Europe, or in bone-dry LA and Las Vegas. In such a hot climate the water wastage is shocking, the more so since sprinkling is used wastefully.

As jobs have moved into cities, so have the property speculators, many of them foreign. The younger generation and new workforce have difficulty in finding accommodation, much of which is treated as assets and kept empty. Affordable housing is hard to come by, so people rent. Unfortunately for the young and the new working population, rented accommodation earns its money from the tourist months and empties in the winter. If

High-rise living in Nicosia.

you rent in the "cold" months, you may need to move out by June and come back in October.

Socializing is not what is used to be—neighbor with neighbor, and children playing in the streets, never out of sight of a familiar pair of eyes. Urbanization, Cypriots notice, brings a loss of proximity, a loss of politeness, and stress. Through Western eyes, though, the Cypriots still enjoy a comfortably humane pace of life, as parents and children still live near each other, if not just around the corner, and much of the workforce has time to go home for lunch. The size of the island also means that usually no one is more than a three-hour drive away.

TOWN AND VILLAGE

Until very recently daily life meant that the family lived very close to each other because the population was concentrated in villages. In those not-so-distant days everybody knew everybody, as the saying goes. Now two-thirds of the population is urban. Consequently the village link is weakening as people migrate to towns or abroad. The *patrikó*— the ancestral home with its garden or land—is sold or broken up among the heirs. Thousands of Diaspora Cypriots have built a family holiday home. Thousands have returned to retire. The difference now is that most have invested near the coast. The Diaspora children and grandchildren of the older

The village of Kato Drys in Larnaca District, bathed in early morning light.

generation are happy to enjoy holiday breaks in the old country, with its free and comfortable accommodation, though few are keen to visit the old village to explore the family landscape.

The big exodus of village depopulation occurred in the 1970s, when more than 35 percent of the population became permanent refugees. Tens of thousands of displaced Cypriots, most of them from an agrarian background, left the country altogether. Many Greek Cypriots kept the keys to their lost homes, even though they may have emigrated as far as Australia or the USA. In the South, new homes had to be built for them, thereby accelerating urbanization.

The Turkish Cypriots, who comprised 18 percent of the island's population, had fewer refugees. This

Traditional house and paved street in the village of Lefkara.

meant there were more than enough Greek houses in
the North to provide accommodation for the Turkish
Cypriots, as well as for the thousands of settlers.

The shift from country to town is so recent that
Cypriots identify their origin by their parental
village. The younger, urban-born generation will
more readily identify with their town of birth.

THE DAILY ROUND

Cypriots prefer not to skip meals and don't like to
treat them as an occasion for quick snacks. Breakfast
at its best and healthiest consists of fresh, uncooked
produce and dairy. It can include grilled halloumi

cheese, eggs, *lountza* (Cypriot sausage), *anari* (soft white cheese), fresh fruit and yogurt with honey, olives, and fresh sesame buns from the local bakery. It is often a large meal because lunch is eaten as late as three in the afternoon. Midday in Cyprus means two or three o'clock. Until then, they may have a *boúkoma*, a snack. Convenience Western breakfasts are on the rise.

Schools are often nearby and, together with public services, start between 7:30 and 8:00 a.m. Often the grandparents take over the parental household and take the children to school, and hand over the reins when the parents return.

Shops open at varying hours from 7:00 a.m., but usually after 8:30 a.m., and can close as late as 9:00 p.m. It depends on the location, with tourist areas remaining open longer. Saturdays and Sundays see shorter opening hours. Bakeries may bake and serve round the clock. Half-day closing is still observed by some shops on Wednesdays and Saturday afternoons.

A point to bear in mind. In Cyprus certain imported products—such as shoes, cereals, confectionery, condiments, or washing-up liquids—that have exactly the same label as in other parts of Europe and are made by the same companies, do not feel the same. They are not fakes and they have not been altered by local climatic conditions. Around 22 percent of branded products marketed as being identical will have different ingredients. That is because the manufacturer will produce the same

Setting up the stand at Nicosia's municipal wholesale fruit and vegetable market.

product but of a lesser quality, depending on the country of its destination.

Weekly shopping for fresh seasonal produce can be done amid the lively banter and visual delights of local weekly markets, or at outlets outside town that provide good parking facilities. In market halls the earlier you go the better. Take your time examining and comparing produce. Feel free to ask where it originates from and to sample.

Lunch is taken well after one or two o'clock; those who can, take a siesta at home in the heat of the day, but the public sector and bank employees head home after 3:00 p.m. The main meal is usually supper, after

107

seven in the evening, because that is when the family can get together. Increasingly nowadays it is a light meal, but not if you have guests or are dining out.

Twenty-four-hour television and live programs from Greece and Turkey can remain on all day for those at home and be switched off as the household returns.

Where applicable, women will invariably be responsible for the hiring, timetabling, and duties of domestic staff.

CIVIL SERVANTS

Cypriots across the island can take pride in the fact that their country's civil service is rooted in the Anglo-Saxon system. In the South it is required that civil servants remain apolitical in their work. However, they are allowed to stand for political office. If elected, they have to resign. If they are not elected and wish to resume their job, they need to take forty days' leave in order to shed their political frame of mind.

On the one hand, it is easy to access government-owned public utilities such as electricity, water, or banking. On the other, bureaucracy is cumbersome. Jobs are for life, "unless you kill someone and then you are fired," joked one senior civil servant. There are not many older faces in the civil service since early and full retirement can be drawn at fifty-five, now pushed to fifty-eight for those who joined after 2005. As a customer, your urgent priorities will not draw much sweat from the foreheads of public officials. It is not an ethos that brooks contradiction or admits to mistakes.

A frank, no-nonsense, government-initiated report was commissioned "to improve the effectiveness and efficiency of the public sector and thereby offer all citizens better services." The old bugbear known as *rousféti* featured. Despite a clear consensus on the need to change things, it remains, according to the report, difficult to eliminate fully because it is driven by both patrons and their clients. On the other hand, the Republic of Cyprus ranks among those countries less affected by corruption, despite local perceptions to the contrary.

TO *ROUSFÉTI* OR NOT

Rousféti is an Ottoman word widely applicable in the region and probably in most countries. It involves a form of political patronage that determines appointments, promotions, and occasionally the allocation of a public contract. It relies on a system of reciprocal favors that create an obligation between two people; it does not involve an exchange of money. *Rousféti* mostly affects the public sector. When you have a patron, you do not need proof of high performance and this demotivates more deserving personnel.

How does it work in ordinary life if you need a favor? Apparently "you make the right phone call." Who to in particular? There is no *rousféti* directory.

It is an ironic coincidence that one of the plays brilliantly adapted into the Cypriot dialect is Gogol's *Diary of a Madman*, about a tormented, low-ranking civil servant always blaming others.

GROWING UP IN CYPRUS

In many ways, children have never had it so good. They are loved and doted upon and granted much leeway. Parents strive to provide them with a car, an apartment, perhaps a credit card. If they go out with friends, rather than walk home or catch a bus, they can expect mum or dad to come and pick them up by car. The younger ones are not expected to share home chores; even for the older ones to help with housework can be seen as undignified by society. As one teenager explained, clearing up the dishes and having your *yiayia* (grandmother) tell your friends what a good boy you are does not enhance your street cred.

Children tend to go to bed late, especially if there are guests, and will often eat separately on such occasions. To see them, you'd think they are encouraged to run around, bringing dizziness and positive energy to the house. The family structure and underlying discipline ensures that children will not go feral. With time, they will pick up the torch to contribute to family ceremonies.

Many mothers will refer to their children as "my baby," especially the boys, right up to adulthood.

They will proudly inform their friends that "my baby did …," even if the "baby" in question has just clinched a major deal. Such doting will occasionally prompt an exasperated father to say "Woman, have you seen your baby? He's a grown man with his own family!" The expression "my child" can be used by a much older person, especially by a woman, to address or advise a clearly younger person, even if they don't know them.

In truth, good prospects for young people are a bit thin; salaries in 2022 could be as low as €400 a month. This is mitigated by the fact that many have somewhere parental to stay. The Covid 19 pandemic did little to improve their chances of work, and many have had to move abroad. Since the 1990s they have been leaving as young professionals with diplomas in their hands, some perchance dreaming of following in the footsteps of Nicosia-born Sir Christopher Pissarides and, like him, winning the Nobel Prize in Economics. At home, mixed marriages are increasing; however, the Greek Orthodox Church will not condone marriage to someone of a different religion, and spouses from different Christian denominations will need to be baptized Orthodox.

EDUCATION, EDUCATION, EDUCATION

One cannot overestimate the importance Cypriots attach to the education of their children, right through to university and postgraduate studies.

Consequently, the country enjoys a highly educated, English-speaking labor force that makes it a sought-after destination for so many companies—as well as being cheaper. Cypriots who go abroad for postgraduate degrees often end up finding skilled jobs abroad. Education is compulsory between the ages of five and fifteen.

Many children attend a *frondistírio*, a private cramming school or test preparation center, outside school hours to ensure they achieve the best results for university entry. This incurs an extra expense. Some question the need for this supplement because school should be good enough, and also because it encourages children to skip classes in the knowledge that they can catch up at the *frondistírio*.

Private schools generally enjoy a higher reputation. Classes are smaller, children receive more attention, and are said to behave better. There is no need for *frondistírio*. They also teach both in Greek and in English. Some Cypriots believe it is best for their children to attend a state school for the first years during the *demotikó* (primary or grade school, grades 1–6) in order to consolidate their Greek language. Various foreign communities have opened their own schools, most of which are also attended by Cypriots. In such a small country, their cosmopolitan *paréa* is noticeable.

State schooling and higher education are paid for by taxes. There are also private schools and universities that the state does not usually cover. The recently established University of Cyprus is rising at

an impressive rate in world ranking. It has benefited
from large financial donations as well as major
archival collections.

For centuries, Greek schooling had depended
on the Church until the nineteenth century, when
mainland Greek teachers, many of them women,
were sent. Quite an adventure for these ladies.
Schools were funded by private individuals and
still bear their names. In the twentieth century, the
Turkish Republic sent its own teachers. In both cases
children absorbed the national cultural values of the

The historic Phaneromeni high school in Nicosia, soon to house the University of
Cyprus' School of Architecture.

so-called mother countries and continue to do so to this day. Children feature prominently in the national celebrations of all communities.

While universities in the Republic of Cyprus are mostly attended by Greek-Cypriot and exchange students, they also accept Turkish-Cypriot students if they meet the criteria; they also generate income from foreign students. Turkish-Cypriot universities, on the other hand, consist of 30 percent mainland Turkish students, just over 18,000. For anyone interested, it is best to check which have international accreditation; some opened to attract paying students from Africa and Asia. The largest and leading university, the Near East University in north Nicosia, is owned by one man and hosts an annual music festival.

NATIONAL SERVICE

Cyprus is one of the most militarized places in the world. National service in both communities aims to enforce social cohesion round a strongly nationalist theme. For both, the opponent is visible across the Green Line.

The Cypriot National Guard (it does not carry the rubric "Greek") is reinforced by two mainland Greek Army infantry battalions. Military service is mandatory for all male citizens and for non-citizens born to a Greek-Cypriot parent. They are liable from the age of sixteen for a fourteen-month term and

Greek-Cypriot conscripts on parade for military Oath Day.

remain as reservists, called up yearly for one or two days until their fiftieth birthday.

In the TRNC, operational control of the "Turkish Cypriot Security Force" is believed to come under the Turkish forces. At the age of eighteen Turkish-Cypriot men are liable for a twenty-four-month service, which can be bought out for a moderate monetary fee. Discharged soldiers serve in the reserves until they reach fifty.

CHAPTER SIX

TIME OUT

In its leisure, entertainment, and arts Cyprus is experiencing a reawakening, and it is fascinating to see how this lively nation chooses to engage with the modern world. This is not the island of Lawrence Durrell's *Bitter Lemons.*

One Cypriot who has lived abroad—so many have—and who runs her own company there, observed about her compatriots that most in her circle are educated and refined in surprising ways, but culturally a little insular. Cypriot high society— in the sense of those who are wealthy, influential, and cultured in a so-called European way—saw the island as the Cinderella of the arts world and are only gradually making it their home. For instance, it did not grow along the same pathways as Malta or Corfu, which were also ruled by Frankish kings and Britain. Though those two islands are considerably smaller, they have long enjoyed their own opera houses and once hosted a lively opera scene that made them a must-stop destination for many a rising diva or international orchestra. Today Cyprus is the new kid in town, and there is enough to miss out on when you leave.

LEISURE

The quality of one's leisure is important in a country that enjoys a good work–life balance. All employees are entitled to paid leave for at least four weeks per year. Many take some in July and August, especially since school holidays are from mid-June to early September, and up to fifteen days for Christmas and Easter. When Cypriots want to take a wild, one-night break from life's chores, they become Greek, as in Zorba the Greek. They go to the *bouzoúkia*, those nightclubs where popular urban Greek music is played live and plates are smashed at the feet of impassioned dancers. During the tourist season, Cypriots mostly go to the Greek islands. Turkish Cypriots choose coastal Turkey.

They like doing things in groups when young, visiting former university friends abroad or inviting them over. Later in life, trips are with the family.

For centuries Greek Cypriots have been visiting the Holy Land on pilgrimages. They take with them gifts and consumables for the many, time-old Greek Orthodox monasteries and churches there and bring back blessings and holy items.

Gambling is not an unusual pastime. Some cafés have back rooms where unlicensed gambling takes place; the owners and players are supposedly fined if caught. However, there are stories of Greek Cypriots addicted to gambling who lose fortunes in the casinos of the North. The financial benefits for the North were so vast that it relaxed border procedures so as not to put off punters.

The uplands have become a favorite for their cool air and breathtaking views, and winter skiing. The best place to stretch one's legs is the Troodos Mountains, which are also dotted with hidden villages and especially with lovely country tavernas.

YOUTH AND THE YOUNG IN SPIRIT

The young trendy scene is readily found, ranging from thudding music to silky resorts such as "Napa" (Ayia Napa). A world of fancy(ish) bars, coffee shops, and juice bars. Days of sunbathing by the pool and going round the corner for pancakes and ices as the beach-girls finally decide to head for the sea where the wind blows the waves white and blue. The boys sip their frappé coffee, sitting around tables and communicating via social platforms with each other and with improvised friends who are sitting at other tables in other countries. "How things have changed," wonders the older generation. Cypriot social media is quick to respond that not all youth action and inaction is about being "mindless." Far from it. There is acro yoga, tennis, gym, socializing, more swimming, diving, SUP, beach rackets, and hikes and camping for the adventurous. It depends on what one is seeking. Yes, people do go to bars, but they also appreciate good food, and drink coffee and fall into philosophical conversations.

In small out-of-the way dives tucked away in the half-deserted lanes of old Limassol or Nicosia, one can be drawn in by the cool sounds of classic rock; these are the *barákia,* a place where friends find time to meet a new face, pick a *mezé* from their plate, follow the smoke that rises from their cigarette, and pursue conversations that extend into the early hours of the morning before the shop owners around the corner roll up the blinds and sprinkle the sidewalks with water in anticipation of another warm day.

Across the island and from the Diaspora, families come and go on excursions, creating good memories of picnics, fun, sea, *mezé*, wine, nature, and breaking into song.

THESE SHOES ARE NOT MADE FOR WALKING

Walking for pleasure is a mystery in many parts of the world. Cyprus is no exception. There needs to be a practical purpose for two-legged locomotion, the most obvious being to get from A to B, or walking about the house to do things. There is *vólta*, described earlier, strolling along the promenade to push the baby buggy, to guide the young child in its first steps, or to mix with one's fellow citizens. There is walking for work—the shepherd, the waiter, the laborer, the policeman, the patrolling soldier. And, of course, there is walking across the parking lot to get into the car. The very idea of trekking seems eccentric here. But lately there are plenty of enthusiasts across the island.

HOME COOKING AND *HAUTE CUISINE*

If love passes through the stomach, then the love for Cyprus grows through its delicious, healthy home produce. This is not a reference to the variety and quality of its world cuisine, or to its holiday resort food of standardized American and Middle Eastern plates,

Light lunch: grilled halloumi cheese and salad.

Left: Watermelon and tangy feta cheese. *Right:* Lokma, or Loukoumades, a bite-sized doughnut drenched in honey, particularly popular during Ramadan.

all served with French fries. It can be tempting to settle for a quick burger takeout. Fortunately, it is also easy to go out and buy excellent true home cooking.

Cypriots will joke that "Cypriots are always tired and hungry," or that "the essentials of life are *poúga* and *skembé*"—Cypriot dialect for wallet and stomach. Food is a lifestyle. Cypriot dishes offer refreshing ingredients to counterbalance the summer heat. There are plenty of different, cooling seasonal salads and fruit. Since it is a hot but fertile country, raw vegetables are much appreciated—cucumbers, parsley, olives, mild little onions, coriander sprigs, slices of kohlrabi (cabbage turnip), often as entrées or to accompany the main meal.

The islanders are strong on nuts, pulses, lentils, *koukiá* (local fava beans), *louviá* (black eye beans). These are traditionally served lightly boiled on their own with a sprig of something thrown on top; even businessmen will buy different pulse dishes for lunch. There is still a healthy resistance to processed foods. Schoolchildren will not rush "for chips and crap," commented a Cypriot father. Having said that, Cyprus potatoes enjoy the highest reputation due to the rich, red soil in which they grow. *Kolokási* is the native mild-flavored potato-like root vegetable—an acquired taste, dating back to the Roman Empire.

Takeout grills are becoming more numerous. It is uncomplicated and convenient to throw meats over a grill. Cypriots do like their meat, especially the local specialties of Cypriot *lougániko* (sausage), *lountza*, a delicacy of dried pork, and *tsamarella*, salted and cured lamb. And of course, grilled *sheftaliá*, thickly cut chunks of meat mixed with plenty of parsley and wrapped in transparent caul fat. You can measure the kitchen skills of a household by the quality of its home prepared *sheftaliá* when they hold a *soúvla* (barbecue). Curiously for an island, Cyprus is not strong on fish.

Cypriot olive oil is much prized. In the days of the Roman Empire, the island was one of the main suppliers for Rome. Some of its olive trees are reputed to be nine hundred years old, still leafy and hollowed out by time, providing enough room to sit in on a chair. However, Cypriot cuisine is not heavy on oil.

It is not usual to recommend the lemons of a country. The green Cypriot lemons of late spring/ early summer are in a rare, different league from the yellow ones. They have a subtle fruity sweetness that goes well with most dishes and presents *aficionados* with the temptation to tuck into their pulp.

If you are offered food when you are not hungry, the polite thing is to accept a little as an acknowledgment of the hospitality. Empty hands and an empty plate stand out awkwardly.

There is a great variety of sweets. Five hundred years ago, Cyprus was a leading producer of cane sugar before European production was taken over by the New World. Local specialties owe much to Byzantine and Ottoman inventiveness with filo pastry, honey, and nuts. How to resist a nutty *baklava* or stringy *kadaífi*? Also, preserved candied fruit in syrup served on a small plate are a must, especially if homemade. In the North, the green walnut *macun* in its own syrup is to die for. *Tahinópita* made with tahini is another favorite. And then there is the carob, neglected in the West, which gives a chocolate-like taste to biscuits, liquor, syrups, and cakes. (Or, since it has been around since biblical times, one could say chocolate feels and tastes a bit like carob.)

Whereas the South relies on herbs and has been influenced by Western cuisine in all its ups and downs, the North over the last decades has absorbed Turkish cuisine. One obvious sign is that Northern cooked food is usually darker because of the use of spices. This new distinction is a product of the division. The Greek- and Turkish-Cypriot communities in London are a living example of how food united them; their native supermarkets still offer the same old country produce, including one of word's favorite cheeses, halloumi, and are busy with customers from both communities.

Cypriot winemaking stretches back to antiquity, with the sweet, amber-colored dessert Commandaria enjoying the oldest pedigree. No doubt a requisite for any self-respecting oenophile, though they can be quite pricey in restaurants.

FLAOÚNA IS CYPRUS

If there is one item that spells "Cyprus" in all its layers, contradictions, and dimensions it has to be the *flaoúna*. From the moment you see it to the moment you take a bite, a question rumbles at the back of your head, "What are you?" Geometrically, it can be a rounded triangle or a squared circle. Is it something stuffed or filled? From your first encounter, it doesn't appear to answer to any generic term. It is baked. Cut it in half and it looks like a bun, or a small loaf with bits in it; one bite and it's a pie, another and it's a pastry. Its ingredients are flour, eggs, mint, sultanas, sugar, salt, halloumi, semolina, full-fat milk (preferably goat's), aromatic *mahleb* grains, mastic powder, sesame seeds, and olive oil. Some of them speak of the West, others of the East.

Flaoúna is eaten in celebration after the dramatic *Anástasis* (Resurrection) liturgy of Holy Saturday,

Freshly baked *flaoúna*.

and thus stands as a hyphen between two worlds
at the most important moment of Cyprus' spiritual
life. It breaks the rigorous fasting of Lent and
announces the dawn of the greatest feast of the year
on Easter Sunday. To Turkish Cypriots it is known
as *pilavuna* and is traditional during Ramadan.

It is labor intensive to make, but not a delicacy.
You can eat it during the year, but how? Sweet or
savory? Meal or accompaniment? Hot-cross bun or
Cornish pasty? It is *flaoúna*, a replenishing specialty
and perfect served with olives, a boiled egg, or
tomato, cucumber, and a sweet Cypriot coffee or
raki. Or just on its own.

TIPPING

Tipping—*filodórima* in Greek or *bahşiş* in Turkish—is not a big deal in Cyprus. The personal decision to tip has now morphed into an often-optional 10 percent service charge in some hotels and restaurants. Customers paying by card may choose to give the 10 percent in cash, lest it ends up in the owner's till rather than going to the wait staff. If paying by cash, they leave the tip separately. If a service charge is not included, it is common courtesy to round up the bill. Bartenders and taxi drivers do not expect a tip, nor do hairdressers; but it is usual to tip delivery persons.

A tour guide may well receive 10 percent above the final bill. You can leave something for the driver, too. As pointed out, when visiting a church one can drop something into the box and light a candle.

ENTERTAINMENT

Entertainment comes out to meet you in Cyprus. Cinema, concerts, live performances, open-air concerts, highbrow, lowbrow, middlebrow. The experience can start from just strolling in the countryside where looking and listening are entertainment. In the villages older men play *távli* (backgammon) at the coffee shop, slapping the checkers on the board and challenging each other to do better, every move and comment followed by a merry band of friends. Along the promenade in the evening you may come across the local post office dance group dressed in Cypriot regalia who have taken over the small, public amphitheater. Then to be followed by a poet reading his latest composition in *tsiatistá,* a style of popular poetry reminiscent of African-American rap but much older, which could be about the return of his modern American cousin to the village. Poetry is important and alive across the island.

Many towns have their own amphitheater. On a much larger scale is the *panegyri,* the festive celebratory day mentioned earlier in the book.

A showstopper is the Carnival of Limassol, in the build-up to Lent, which takes place from late February to March. There are processions, costumes, singing, dancing, drinking, and licensed merrymaking, all culminating in a massive parade with an army of floats.

In central squares in towns, a local organization may organize a festive event to raise public awareness over an issue. There are pop-up stalls of reading materials, books, food, and artisan trinkets. These are occasions to meet new people and listen to impromptu performances. Such open-air cultural festivals, if not organized by them, are welcomed by migrant communities such as Filipinos or Syrians, who embrace the opportunity to share their music and their heritage. That, too, is the new Cyprus.

Post Office workers in Limassol dancing on the Molos promenade.

On the club scene, those away from coastal resorts tend to operate toward the later part of the week, from 10:00 p.m. to 4:00–4:30 a.m. the next day. The staff invariably speak English and are well trained, including professional barmen, to keep up the spirits. There are the Western clubs that get the crowds dancing—sometimes on the tables—with the latest high-energy tracks. The Greek clubs earn their reputation from the big musical acts they invite over from Greece.

The last few years have seen a determined investment in museums, galleries, and new theaters, especially in Nicosia and Limassol, where major productions come from Athens. Theater is subsidized but there is hardly anything in English.

Once a year Paphos, a UNESCO listed World Heritage city, holds the Paphos Aphrodite Festival in late August or early September. The festival features breathtaking performances in the square beside the city's medieval castle and with a view across the sea. Its avidly anticipated Aphrodite Opera Festival invites major international opera companies performing Verdi, Mozart, Rossini. It is packed out.

The Cyprus miracle would have been poorer without the A. G. Leventis Foundation. Major private initiatives have shored up the Cypriot renaissance over the last one hundred and fifty years. Since 1979 the Foundation has given Cypriot culture, history, and tradition a global and permanent presence in the top museums and universities, as well as cofounding the University of Cyprus. In Nicosia it commissioned a modern museum to house the A. G. Leventis Gallery, where three collections of paintings—the Greek, Cyprus, and Paris Collections—showcase artistic developments and cross-influences since the Renaissance. In effect, it gave Cyprus its first national gallery, where Cypriots can enjoy their own legacy with a renewed sense of self-respect. The café-restaurant offers a pretty good brunch or evening drink.

Foreign embassies will have their own cultural programs—anything from exhibitions to concerts or, like the French embassy, a season of excellent free films. Their Web sites share the information with all those interested.

The International Short Film Festival in Limassol in October is a celebrated platform for local and international filmmakers to showcase their work. It covers everything from animation, experimental, to documentary and narrative. Its main target group is fifteen-to-twenty-five-year-olds. These are the bold first steps of a country taking stock of international performances and gearing up to match them. Cyprus is expanding and the arts are benefiting from a new voice.

Across the divide, Greek and Turkish Cypriots keep alive their folk music, which is very much alike and enjoys a wide following. Influences from Greece and Turkey have always enriched the mix.

In Northern Cyprus festivals are rural in nature, with banners often advertising forthcoming events in advance. There are many separate festivals often linked with the harvest of different local produce—the grape, halloumi, carob, date, tulip, orange, walnut. The

Folk dancing at the seasonal *palouze* (grape jelly) festival in the village of Arsos.

strawberry festival allows you to pick your own, and of course there is the harvest festival. They can be seen as quieter versions of the Greek-Cypriot saints' festivals.

One of the most important Northern Cyprus festivals is the annual classical music Bellapais Music Festival, a microcosm of Turkish-Cypriot life. It takes place in May or June at the village of Bellapais, which is perched high above Kyrenia/Girne, around the historic Abbey and surrounded by breathtaking scenery. The festival has hosted performers from many parts of the world and is a showcase for the government of the North and the direction it wishes to take, with sponsorship from its government ministries, local banks, and businesses. Western audiences enjoy the regular participation of Turkish military bands at a classical music festival; their very names succinctly express their purported mission on the island—the "Turkish Armed Forces Harmony Band," the "Band of the Security Forces Command," the "Band Command of Turkish Peace Forces in Cyprus." The festival is accompanied by the Bellapais Silk Cocoon Festival, a product that plays an important role in the North's artisanal industry.

SPORTS

Cypriots were first able to participate in the modern Olympic Games as members of the Greek national team. After independence, they did not have time to organize a bicommunal Olympic team and later efforts did not come through. Cyprus saw its first athletes participate at the 1980 Moscow Olympics. Since then it has won a bronze medal in the men's laser sailing event. It also won thirty-nine medals (and counting) at the Commonwealth Games.

The most popular sports in Cyprus are football (soccer), swimming, and, increasingly, diving. The government has built stadiums, swimming pools, even sports halls, and it subsidizes sports associations and clubs as part of a broader social dialogue. The authorities further ensure that Cyprus' beaches and marinas are repeatedly judged as the cleanest in Europe, with dozens of blue-flag beaches.

The Cypriot government is willing to support the country's outstanding talents. For instance, tennis champion Marcos Baghdatis—ranked No. 20 in the World Association of World Tennis Professionals— was exempted from military service. Financially, the government applies a reduced VAT rate of 5 percent for entry fees at sports events and for fees to use athletic centers.

Hunting and shooting are popular, prompting local and international opposition to the liberties some hunter-poachers take to illegally shoot down thousands of migrating birds.

Football Means Many Things

Football on the island involves, above all, wonderful sport. As an aside, those politically on the right generally support APOEL FC, whose members were active in the uprising against the British in the 1950s. One of their athletes, Michalis Karaolis, was even

An Anorthosis fan celebrates winning the Cypriot Cup in 2021.

hanged by them in 1956 for his involvement and many streets bear his name. APOEL colors are blue for Hellenism and yellow for Byzantium. The left support Omonia FC, which was founded after members of APOEL broke away for political reasons over the Civil War that was raging in mainland Greece. Their colors are green for hope and white for happiness. Most supporters are working-class and believe in Cypriotism, while retaining their identity as Greeks of Cyprus. The two teams are ardent rivals. Anorthosis FC used to be based in Famagusta but had to flee in 1974. It is the team of refugees, and its blue color symbolizes Greece. Even villages used to have two teams, one from the left, one from the right, who would patronize one of the two *kafenío* (traditional, all male-coffee shops), one left, one right.

Sports and Football in Northern Cyprus
The sports associations of Northern Cyprus have not been recognized by international sports-governing

bodies and therefore cannot participate in international games and athletics. There have been initiatives to engage them as fellow players under the umbrella of the Republic of Cyprus, especially since many Turkish Cypriots are employed in the South and receive the same benefits as their fellow Greek Cypriots. But international sports events are inextricably bound up with politics and the question that arises in the North is that if you participate with the South, then are you *de facto* recognizing the sovereignty of the Republic of Cyprus? And for the South, if the North can join international sports governing bodies as an entity does this validate its self-declared statehood?

Many of the Turkish-Cypriot teams fly the Turkish flag on their logo. The leading team is Çetinkaya Türk FC. It was founded in 1930 and became a founding member of the Cypriot First Division in 1934, which included another seven Greek-Cypriot teams. Its colors are yellow and red.

In 2017 Northern Cyprus hosted the CONIFA or Confederation of Independent Football Associations Euro cup. Their teams consisted of unrecognized states and sub-national regions that are excluded from international sports and unaffiliated with FIFA. There were eight participants, including Abkhazia, South Ossetia, and the then reigning champions, Padania, from northern Italy.

Hunting is a popular Turkish-Cypriot pastime and according to local reports more than 10,000 people in the North have hunter licenses and the number of shotguns is over 36,000.

SHOPPING FOR PLEASURE

Cypriots love shopping. There are many small, local shops with that personal touch where people know each other by their first names, or even from childhood. There are shopping malls to get lost in, village markets to light up your senses, even second-hand shops selling anything from chunky old Space Invader video game machines to trendy second-hand clothes. All the latest fashion styles are there. Worth knowing is that one of the many traditional tailors will adjust your household items, your curtains, or sofa coverings in no time and at very competitive prices. If your wallet can take it, bespoke tailors can fit you up, and shoemakers provide you with made-to-measure shoes. There is no harm in asking.

Unique items to bring back from a trip to Cyprus have already been mentioned. Halloumi cheese, carob products (ask at the counter for guidance), preserves. Handmade jewelry and filigree silverwork are much prized, with workshops in the main street, though make sure that anything you buy bears the hallmark of the Cyprus Goldsmiths Association.

Old Venetian Luxury

For a flavor of Venice when it was a sea empire, nothing beats Lefkaritika embroidered linen. During its rule in the fifteenth century, many Venetians lived in Lefkara and passed on their intricate style of embroidery for the governor's court to the local Cypriot women. According to UNESCO, which includes Lefkara laces on its list of intangible cultural heritage, the women fused this with their own ancient Greek and Byzantine patterns and continue to develop these to this day.

Shopping in the North

Shopping in Northern Cyprus is quite a different experience—more Anatolian, with plenty of gift ideas. Silks are high on people's lists, as are scarves, painted tiles, and throws. Turkish pottery, baskets, cushion covers, and handicrafts are perfect as gifts for the home. Most fashion labels spilling out of doorways and into the streets are fake but cheap and worth it if the quality seems steady. Turkish Cypriots in Nicosia often head south on shopping trips, while Greek Cypriots will head north for gasoline, specialist food items, and clothing. Most of the North's shopping venues are in Nicosia, Kyrenia/Girne, and Famagusta/Gazimagusa.

Lefkara lace and traditional embroidery on sale at Pano Lefkara, Larnaca District.

MUST-SEE DESTINATIONS

Cyprus is in a state of constant evolution. One can experience that evolution more intensely when visiting certain sites. The following suggested destinations— and there are many more—are not places where history has stopped, done and dusted. They speak of unfolding business that brings the past to life and relates it to the present.

Kourion Ancient City-State

Kourion sits along a coastal plateau, 330 feet (100 m) above sea level with a commanding view of the Mediterranean. Soon after the Trojan Wars (c. 1260–1180 BCE), Greek families from Argos in the Peloponnese loaded their ships and settled there. Early Christianity brought Kourion its first Basilica. Round the corner, at the ruins of the aptly named Earthquake House, you can guess where the children played, over one and a half thousand years ago. The city was leveled in 648 during the first Arab raids on the island and relocated to nearby Episkopi. The very same commanding heights and ocean winds that brought the ancient Argive ships today make it a heaven for paragliding, while each June its ancient amphitheater hosts Shakespearean plays, in English. Finally, after all these millennia, it is still not part of an independent Cyprus—while supervised by the Cyprus Department of Antiquities, it comes under the SBA of Akrotiri.

The Monastery of Stavrovouni

With its foundation stretching back to Constantine the Great, the key role of this monastery has already been discussed. High above forested valleys and terraced hills, it rests perilously atop what looks like a giant pyramid. It is known as the Mount Athos of Cyprus because no women are allowed. Inside its small church, with its recesses, ancient hagiographies, burning incense, and the psalmody of the monks, you become aware of your location. That there is nothing around and above but the heavens. If you step onto the small balcony jutting out of the church, you stand over a sheer drop and you may wonder what prevents the whole structure from tumbling down. One could say, it is a soaring experience in a place

The Church of All Saints at Stavrovouni.

where the daily goal is to achieve *théosis*, or the ultimate union with God. The material world is far below.

Kyrenia Castle

Wandering about this cavernous fort awakens the child in adults, dreaming to share an adventure. It has not been restored to look like a made-to-measure ruin. It sits on the edge of the tranquil Kyrenia/Girne harbor, a succession of Byzantine, Lusignan, and Venetian walls and towers, wrapped round each other with narrow, unmarked passages between and above them—which is to say, it is not a place for unaccompanied children. How many castles can claim to have seen action within living memory? The British built police barracks in its

Kyrenia Castle. The present walls were built by the Venetians in the sixteenth century over earlier fortifications.

courtyard, then handed it over in 1950 to the Kyrenia Department of Antiquities. Five years later the British authorities used it as a prison for Greek-Cypriot members of EOKA. With independence, the Cypriot National Guard took over, and in 1974 it radioed Nicosia as it came under attack and witnessed across the horizon the arrival of the Turkish invasion force. It became the HQ of the Turkish forces in Cyprus, which, from their dominant position, oversaw the arrival of settlers from mainland Turkey and the flight of its citizens. Now it also houses the famous Kyrenia shipwreck of 288 BCE. The Republic of Cyprus did not let go; it uses the image of the ship on three of its euro coins, as a symbol of all the islanders.

Kykkos Monastery

Set in the Troodos Mountains, this is the most lavish monastery in the country as well as being a major player in the Eastern Orthodox world. One of the routes to Kykkos passes the mountain resort of Platres, home to the novelist Daphne du Maurier in 1936–37, who was enchanted by "the beautiful mountains and the true light of Cyprus."

Akamas

The greatest secret, though, is the rugged peninsula of Akamas, in the northwest, which the British army used for live-fire exercises until 2000. It retains an air of unapproachability, which environmentalists repeatedly defend against official plans to develop it.

CHAPTER SEVEN

TRAVEL, HEALTH, & SAFETY

The infrastructure of Cyprus is good, but public transportation is limited. As a result most people drive. It is one of a handful of countries, such as Britain, Ireland, Malta, and India, where you drive on the left-hand side of the road. You'll need a car to move around. Cycling is still a novelty, but public bicycles are on the increase. Buses are safe and cheap, but run an infrequent service and the last intercity buses may depart in the afternoon. Some routes are worth taking for the scenic experience alone. Buses are popular with poorer immigrants. In Nicosia you can walk through the central bus station and not notice it. The introduction of bus apps enables people, especially teenagers, to catch one without waiting endlessly at bus stops. For a good site to help you plan your trip online go to the links on the Cyprus Tourist Organization Web site, such as the one for buses: motionbuscard.org.cy.

DOCUMENTATION

Many foreign citizens enter simply showing their passport; others receive visas on arrival; some need visas. Naturally, check what applies to you. If you enter the North from Turkey, you may be refused entrance to the South. No vaccinations are needed to enter either part of the island. However, following the Covid-19 pandemic, entry requirements and vaccinations may vary according to circumstance.

If driving, it is advisable to take out insurance. The European Health Insurance Card, EHIC, is valid in the southern Republic of Cyprus and travel insurance and medical coverage is recommended.

Getting Around

Bicycles can be taken on some buses serving the main intercity routes, but no dogs are allowed. Guide dogs might be allowed on buses, in which case they must wear a muzzle and have a health book.

Hiring a vehicle is very easy and the rented cars have red number plates. This is very useful, since Cypriot drivers can be remarkably understanding about the hesitation of foreign drivers.

There is a good taxi service, including shared "service taxis." Make sure the taxi meter is switched on, as airport taxis have been known to cheat. One way this may be done is, when you book a taxi online it does not turn up and then you have to book a more expensive one from the airport.

Rental bicycle station at the Molos seaside park in Limassol.

The British highway code for the SBAs on Cyprus states, "You MUST [*sic*] wait if a train goes by and if the red lights continue to flash." Sadly for enthusiasts, the last train ran in 1951; then the line was pulled up. Happily for rail enthusiasts there is a very informative small railway museum on the slopes of the Troodos Mountains, in Evrychou village.

Since Cypriots are not keen walkers, many households own two or more cars and will drive 300 meters to do the shopping for the convenience of parking in front of the shop. Major traffic jams are standard at certain hours; Limassol and especially Nicosia are notorious for them.

STEPPING BACK IN TIME TO A FRIENDLY LEVANT

In the North, even the tourist office advises that "public transportation is not the most advanced in terms of service and infrastructure." The best way to move around the main arteries of the North are the small, chatty, and very affordable minibuses, also known as "*dolmuş.*" They make up their own timetables and have informal ranks in different parts of any town. They pick up passengers anywhere along the roadside and drop them off wherever they are asked to, as long it is on its route. They do not stray off main roads—an important consideration when planning your visit.

Taxis are not flagged down but found in taxi bays, and fares are negotiable. Tips are not expected.

DRIVING

Driving is on the left. Drivers vary from calm and respectful to aggressive. Pedestrians had better make sure that oncoming cars are stopping before stepping out onto the crosswalk. There are five grades of roads, A (motorways), B (main roads), E (rural roads), F (one lane), and "unclassified." Street signs are very small, if they exist at all, so you might have to stop and ask for directions at local tavernas. On highways the signs for Nicosia will be in the Roman alphabet but will use its Greek name, Lefkosia. If you see a "50 kmph"

(31 mph) speed limit sign, it will be followed by a
"30 kmph" (18 mph) sign, and finally by a "stop" sign,
so no sudden surprises. There can be flash floods,
but none deep enough to bring you to a standstill.

Towns have large central parking lots, but you may
find smaller ones where there is no indication as to
whether a payment must be made. Parking can be a
problem during the busy hours of the day.

Cyprus has one of the highest accident rates in
Europe. If you should be involved in one, the police
may request you to accompany them to the nearest
police station and fill in an accident report. This is a
must for your insurance claim.

The Kindness of Strangers

The first time I hired a car in Cyprus I found myself
lost in one of Nicosia's backstreets, having gone to
buy deliciously baked dishes from a small bakery.
The thought of having to drive blindly up and down
a maze of one-way streets hoping for a chance
encounter with my residence was too upsetting, so
I asked a fellow customer for directions. His wife
and two children were in their car, heading home.
He began explaining, hesitated, then offered, "Just
follow me, I'll take you there." And so it happened
that we zig-zagged onto the main street and he
hooted as we arrived at my destination. Safe and
sound and the food still warm. Such generosity of
spirit was not an exception.

Limassol's split-level Yermasoyia junction.

To date, there are no toll paying roads in Cyprus.

In Northern Cyprus, the intercity roads are wide and comfortable, but once off them conditions can become picturesque. Some roads have not been resurfaced since they were first laid before 1974. For safety, it is advisable not to drive at night, especially with military trucks moving around with dimmed lights. Also, there are some owners of powerful, imported, alpha-male cars who enjoy intimidating driving. New number plates were introduced in 2019 to be recognizable by speed cameras. But many cars have Republic of Cyprus style number plates and the details look as though they've been painted on rather than officially produced. If you are renting, then a "Z" on the number plate singles you out and grants you courtesy and understanding. If you are involved in an accident, immediately contact the vehicle's

insurance company or the car rental agency and file
a police report.

If you intend to drive a vehicle across the Green
Line, make sure you have the relevant insurance
cover and tell the agency if you are hiring. If you
have none, at best you will not be allowed through, at
worst you will, and then the penalties will be huge in
case of a mishap or if you are stopped.

WHERE TO STAY

Republic of Cyprus

Cyprus is a global leader in hospitality. It is in their
DNA to host. Every tourist accommodation in the
South needs to be registered, approved, and classified
by the Cyprus Tourist Organization. You will find
it listed in their easy-to-search *Guide to Hotels And
Other Tourist Establishments*, which is updated online
at visitcyprus.com.

Property investment has gone mostly into coastal,
full-service resort hotels around Ayia Napa, Larnaca,
Limassol, Paphos (which enjoys its own airport),
and the recent development of once languorous
and remote Protaras in the southeast of the island.
Holiday villages with theme parks for the children
are also a favorite, and some are reminiscent in their
architectural quirkiness of Portmeirion in Wales,
but sunny and perfect for swimming.

Air conditioning is compulsory in hotels that
have three stars or more, and in luxury coastal

Luxury resort hotels at Pissouri beach on the south coast.

apartments and villas. Booking is easy online, though you may wish to book smaller hotels in person and try negotiating a price, especially outside the main tourist season. The top end of luxury accommodation has access to private beaches and Cyprus is moving in to capture the private yachting community.

The depopulation of inland villages has led to the growth of agro-tourism as a way of sustaining local life and the environment. It is a gentle form of tourism and educational in a relaxing way.

The Limassol marina can berth a thousand vessels, including ocean-going yachts.

Northern Cyprus

Northern Cyprus would like to but does not rely on European tourism, not least because of the international trade embargo and the contested ownership of many properties. More than 70 percent of annual arrivals come from Turkey and fewer than 80,000 visitors are from Europe. Compare this with the government-controlled Republic of Cyprus, which sees 2.8 million tourist arrivals from Europe and Russia alone. Of course, the Covid pandemic affected numbers and hit local shopkeepers.

Northern Cyprus is specifically geared to holiday resort accommodation, mostly along the idyllic central section of the northern coast, with Kyrenia/Girne as its center, and then around Famagusta/Gazimagusa in the east. The North has the best natural beaches on the island, especially along the many coastal stretches where there has been no development. Some of them are so isolated that you may wish to skinny dip; but it's best not to, out of respect for local sensitivities. There is a slow diversification toward eco and agricultural tourism. For those content with more rural lettings, they will enjoy a slower, less stressful style of life if they don't expect too much.

Kyrenia's historic harbor is lined with cafés, bars, and restaurants.

Hotel standards vary, since the government has no control over them. Some luxury hotels away from the beaches specialize in offering room service and everything you can eat and drink with optional pampering; they are popular with customers from the South. Turkish-Cypriot hospitality is warm. The service is well meaning but English is not widely spoken. Hotel rates are lower than in the South.

Many of the new hotels are run or built by mainland Turkish investors on Greek-Cypriot-owned land whose owners fled. This does not affect the services offered. Since the late 1990s much hotel accommodation caters to the considerable numbers involved in gambling and sex tourism, and these are therefore inappropriate for women visitors and families. A new form of resort, referred to as conservative or Halal tourism, caters to religiously observant sensitivities, offering separate beaches for the sexes and no alcohol.

HEALTH AND SAFETY

Cyprus has both a public health care system provided by central government and a private health sector. It is easily accessible and reasonably good. The 1960 state model of the British colonial era was replaced in 2019 by a general health care system that allows for competition by public and private providers. Specialists can be accessed directly without needing a referral from a general practitioner. EU citizens and permanent residents in Cyprus are eligible for state health care; non-EU citizens need private health care, which is relatively affordable. Cyprus has six public general hospitals, a modern oncology center, and more than seventy private hospitals and health-care clinics. Occasionally users of the system observe that some doctors do not keep up to date with medical advances and some practices are not up to scratch. As usual, it is advisable to choose by recommendation.

VAT is at the reduced rate of 5 percent on pharmaceutical products and on vaccines used for the health care of humans or animals.

Many Cypriots go abroad for their health issues, in particular to the UK and Athens, where there may be relatives they can rely upon. Israeli hospitals with their specializations have lately been added to their list.

For dental work, some Cypriots from the South choose to head north to dentists who can offer good work and at a lower price.

The health system coped as well as can be expected with the Covid-19 pandemic and people respected the safety measures required of them. Vaccination centers were clean, organized, with only small lines, and the personnel were helpful. Occasionally, the only glitch was a lack of dual ventilation systems.

LOW CRIME BUT . . .

Compared to other European countries, Cyprus, both North and South, has low crime rates. Nevertheless, one should take the normal precautions against opportunistic crime. There are some scams and petty thefts. The number of burglaries is low, and thieves target empty or easy-to-enter properties.

On a different scale, there is the issue of persons subjected to forced prostitution and labor. Media reports and human rights groups concur with reports by the US Overseas Security Advisory Council that "The government-controlled Republic of Cyprus (ROC) is a destination for sex trafficking, which occurs in private apartments and hotels, on the street, and within commercial sex outlets."

In the North, prostitution is illegal, but those who profit from the exploitation include persons in important positions. The report notes that "In the unrecognized 'Turkish Republic of Northern Cyprus,' sex trafficking is a significant problem. Nightclub workers, who live at the clubs, regularly report that employers seize their passports, leaving them little freedom of movement. Groups vulnerable to forced labor include domestic workers, asylum seekers, and foreign migrants working in the construction and agricultural sectors." In both cases the law is quite insufficient while the criminal gangs involved are very efficient.

It should be stressed that women feel safe across Cyprus and just need to take all the usual precautions. In the conservative North single women are not usually chatted up out of the blue, and in the South this usually happens in holiday resorts where it is often par for the course, both ways.

Organized crime, not least involving foreigners, has involved shootings, car bombings, arson attacks, even against courthouses. Extreme, politically motivated attacks have targeted media establishments. But this does not affect those outside these criminal circles.

SECURITY IN MILITARY ZONES, NO PHOTOGRAPHY

Cyprus is broadly divided into four areas, namely the government South, the Turkish-Cypriot North, the British SBAs, and lastly, the UN-controlled buffer zone, or Green Line (which itself consists of zones within zones). The UN military zone is a demilitarized area and extends approximately 112 miles (180 km) across the island; its width varies from a few meters in Nicosia to a few kilometers elsewhere. Its northern and southern limits are the lines where the Greek and Turkish belligerents stood following the ceasefire of August 16, 1974, as recorded by the UN Peacekeeping Force In Cyprus (UNFICYP).

In the eastern part of the island, the British Sovereign Base Area of Dhekelia replaces the UN buffer zone. At its narrowest, the SBA zone separating "Turkish-Cypriot North" from "Greek-Cypriot South" consists only of a smooth, dual-lane road, the E303, which is 6 miles (10 km) long. How narrow is it? If you were to allow little George to

A truncated road in Nicosia ending at the Green Line. At this point the buffer zone is 70 feet (50 meters) wide.

answer nature's call off the left lane, he waters the Turkish side; off the right lane and he waters the Greek side; on the road and it is all British.

So here are the areas within the buffer zone. Entry to most of them is forbidden for non-UN personnel. The zone is a haven for native flora and fauna because there is no human dumping or interference. UNFICYP prides itself on preserving the natural life cycle. Then there are those parts where farming can take place and civilians have free access. Also, there are several villages or special areas (called Civil Use Areas), where more than 10,000 people live and/or work, and there is the "wild west" Pyla (see page 61). Finally, scattered throughout the buffer zone, you will see abandoned villages of crumbling houses, hollowed-out shops, barns, and places of worship.

UNFICYP keeps a 24/7 watch over the buffer zone, ready to intervene. It records and handles around 1,000 incidents each year, "from name-calling to unauthorized use of firearms." The area remains heavily mined.

Wherever you see the sign "No Photography," observe it, because someone will be observing you and will take action. Wherever there are signs along military areas to reduce speed, reduce it.

The advice about Turkish military camps is, avoid them; do not slow down alongside them; do not take any pictures or hold a camera or make any stops. On a different note, Turks revere their flag. Northern Cyprus is probably the only place where even the Google Earth camera vehicle has a Turkish flag visibly displayed on its hood.

A "Pirate" Returns to Cyprus

The director of the film *Pirates of the Caribbean—Dead Man's Chest* wanted the two sailors quarreling over the hero's hat to invent a language. They happened to be Jimmy Roussounis, a Greek Cypriot and Nej Adamson Salih, a Turkish Cypriot, who chose to shout at each other in their respective Greek-Cypriot and Turkish-Cypriot dialects. This is the only time the two dialects have been used together in a Hollywood film.

London-born Roussounis is happy at how the new Cyprus is shaping up. He lives in Limassol, where he runs a residential development company with his half-French wife, commuting to England as acting parts turn up. He is a committed member of the Cyprus Academic Dialogue, a "bi-communal NGO of academics and scholars engaging for peace in their shared island."

After the unrecognized border had opened up for crossings, he made a beeline to a village in Northern Cyprus to meet the Turkish-Cypriot refugees who used to live in his paternal village in the South, Páno Aródes, above Paphos. The Turkish-Cypriot neighbors were not chased out in fear because this mixed village had been very integrated and the separation was a traumatic event for all. As soon as the older Turkish Cypriots saw him, they recognized his father in his features and greeted him with open arms.

Roussounis could live in England or France but chose Cyprus because, as they say, you can do two or three things in a day; it is not a *fasaría*, a slog. You can go off into the mountains in the morning, have lunch, come back for a swim in the afternoon, and watch a small opera performance in the evening. His teenage children go to a private, English-language school, and the wide mix of people introduces them to a cosmopolitan environment while being grounded in their Cypriot roots.

CHAPTER EIGHT

BUSINESS BRIEFING

THE ECONOMY

Cyprus has an open economy that has proved to be resilient, expanding since the 1990s when it assessed the requirements and opportunities of a possible EU membership, to which it acceded in 2004. The country presents itself as an EU outpost, an investment hub, and a logistics center.

Until the banking crisis of 2013 it had one of the fastest growing economies in Europe and the country thought it would become the Tiger Economy of the eastern Mediterranean. Then the financial crisis meant that the money its banks had received from being a tax haven, especially from the Russians, had been invested in huge shares of the Greek sovereign debt. When Greece was hit by a catastrophic debt crisis, Cyprus followed, and its massive debt was met largely by ordinary Cypriot depositors. Soon the banks diversified, and the country slowly started implementing reforms suggested by the EU and the World Bank. As a quick and easy solution to its need for liquidity, the government introduced the selling of Cypriot—and in effect EU—citizenship to those able to invest 2 million euros each. It cashed in over 8 billion euros. The "citizenship for investment program" enriched many a Cypriot company handling and charging for the process, but it ended in 2020.

As the economy was getting back on its feet the Covid-19 pandemic struck, bringing growth to a halt; however, the government swiftly moved in with support packages, including for the "cross-border" Turkish-Cypriot workforce.

Today public debt is around 26 billion euros and unemployment has been floating at 9 percent.

Cyprus is an international business center with high professional services and top regional advisors, which offers a secure and stable EU environment in a troubled part of the world. Occasionally it draws to its shores media attention over "dodgy money" stories. In a move to attract non-EU investment, it has established the Fast Track Business Action Mechanism for non-EU nationals. Foreign direct investment is absorbed by banking, shipping—where Cyprus has the largest crew management center in the world—and real estate.

In response to the importance of tourism, Cyprus now has a dedicated Ministry of Tourism to attract year-round visitors. Its luxury tourism sector in particular is concentrating on conferences, health tourism, pampering and wellness, and holiday villages. A giant Hong Kong-owned company aims to build the largest integrated casino resort in Europe.

The country's greatest export market is the European Union, and it enjoys healthy trading relations with Greece, the UK, Libya, the Marshall Islands, the Netherlands, and France. Suppliers of goods are Greece, Italy, the UK, Germany, Israel, and China. Many Greek Cypriots realize they could do very lucrative business with Turkey, but the situation on the island makes it impossible. Turkey bans Cypriot-flag vessels from entering its ports.

THE DISCOVERY OF GAS OFF APHRODITE'S ISLAND

Dame Fortune was mischievous in placing within reach of the island huge amounts of natural gas. A great advantage of having access to gas that could be branded as Cypriot is that it can be sold without restrictions in Europe. So now Cyprus' business community aims to turn the country into the energy hub of Europe—if it becomes a producer. But hydrocarbons are an entirely new kind of business that needs new knowledge and new skills, with which the population and universities of Cyprus are not up to speed. It will need secure storage facilities, gas processing plants, the servicing of supply vessels, repair, and maintenance. The foreign examples it can learn from are Aberdeen, Stavanger, and Baku, with their offshore gas fields; but these places do not have to juggle gas with a coastal tourism that contributes 22 percent to the Cypriot GDP.

In any case, the Turkish side disagrees. At first it had contended that the Greek-Cypriot fossil fuel plans excluded a fair deal with the Turkish Cypriots. Ankara then expanded the maritime areas it surveyed for Turkish gas. Why? This was part of its wider strategy "to challenge the delimitation of the Exclusive Economic Zone and the continental shelf between the Republic of Cyprus and its neighboring States," according to the RoC government. Cyprus then strengthened its military ties with Israel, the UAE, and Egypt. The country is entering uncharted waters. So for now Cypriot hydrocarbon reserves will remain where Mother Nature intended them, tucked below the seabed.

FROM LOCALISM TO INTERNATIONALISM

Business in Cyprus is based upon relationships that develop slowly. Whether it is localism, parochialism, or just a good old-fashioned need to get to know the people who enter your life, the building of long-term relationships is very important. Your potential partners will wish to meet your family, if applicable, to have an idea of where you are coming from, what sort of a person you are. This fosters loyalty and bonds. Therefore, socializing with your counterparts plays an important role.

Until the 1990s the typical business outlook was very local, with an attitude of "If it ain't broke, don't fix it," mainly because the economy was locally based on agriculture and the export of minerals. While localism remains paramount, the island has gained the self-confidence to position itself as an investment gateway to the EU and as an international springboard for opportunities in the Middle East. Cypriots had been gaining ever-wider experience of both these geographic regions since the 1960s, through their maritime sector and through the investments and interactions of their own companies. They then marketed that regional knowledge internationally, having received a huge impetus from the new technologies and the volume of Cypriot students graduating from foreign universities to staff them.

HIERARCHY AND MANAGEMENT STYLE

Business involves people, and where there are people anywhere in Cyprus there is a hierarchy. As with Cypriot families, it is important to show respect to people in senior positions and your older counterparts. How is respect shown? This is not about bowing or smiling. If anything, a serious, or poker, face is best. Forced social smiling is a cultural trait alien to Cypriots.

The senior person will talk the most, and usually no one will interrupt until discussions open up to external ideas and suggestions. In such a setup, there will be no criticism of anyone or of your counterparts, no open disagreement. Accept it when respect is shown to you; do not tell anyone, "Please don't stand on ceremony." Such an attitude does no one a favor because indirectly you are telling them that respect for *their* position is artificial. It implies you are challenging the concept that who you know is more important than what you know. If no one respects anyone's place then the whole structure collapses. However, you can later enter into a more informal style of discussion with persons of equivalent rank.

Hierarchy means that a number of influential local families remain on top, produce presidents of the Republic, and are treated like royalty. Impressive university degrees or professional achievements do not easily open doors to Cypriot companies. As we have seen, to cut through hierarchies, particularly in the public sector, there is *rousféti*—an informal arrangement whose beneficiaries are not exposed (see page 59).

BUSINESS ETIQUETTE

Err on the side of formality. Casual dress, jeans, and trainers are out; even suit separates are a little daring. Smart trousers and a crisp shirt are fine for more relaxed meetings. Otherwise go for a dark, conservative business suit. Women will wear a conservative skirt. There will be occasions to dress casually, though follow the lead of your Cypriot business partners. In Nicosia, where the government and embassies are, you would need to add a tie.

Timekeeping is more flexible here. Remember that in Cyprus, in a general context, "midday" does not mean twelve noon but something between 1:00 p.m. and 3:00 p.m. Likewise, appointments are not on the dot, but a ten-to-fifteen-minute slot when your counterpart may arrive. However, it is a matter of courtesy for an outsider to be punctual. Make an appointment in advance. Do not text to confirm. If you are there first, when you meet, stand up, shake hands, keep eye contact, even ask how the family are doing if they have been mentioned in a previous meeting or if you have met them. You can exchange general information before getting down to the business at hand and do not be surprised if the meeting occasionally veers off the agreed agenda or the main topic.

MEETINGS

Cypriots prefer face-to-face meetings, especially if in Cyprus. The initial request is usually done in writing or by e-mail and can be followed up and confirmed by telephone, or you can first call the secretary to express your intention, and then e-mail. The success of the online meetings that were forced on the whole world during the pandemic did slightly weaken the preference for personal meeting. Even so, online meetings are considered second-best. Video conferencing with other partners is perfectly acceptable if your Cypriot colleague initiates it in your presence for practical reasons.

The value placed on personal relations means that if you are a representative and your company replaces you, the loyalty to you will not be automatically transferred to it. So, in a way, it's back to square one if you have been the only company face.

Meetings are friendly. You won't feel like a cog in the machine, if only because the personal relationships are central in business life. The company is often treated as a second family or even an extension of the family if owned by one of its members. If you have had previous interactions or relevant friendships with Cypriots, it is good to seek advice from them about finding someone who can help you navigate your first local steps.

Usually first names are used when speaking to foreigners in English. The same people will introduce newcomers by their title followed by their surname.

NEGOTIATIONS

Come thoroughly prepared. Concessions are achievable, but not if you criticize what someone is saying, as this makes it personal, and the personal sticks. Don't rush—clarity trumps speed. It is not inappropriate to pause before you speak—it shows you are considering a point. During negotiations straightforward language will be used. Pronounced accents might affect the intelligibility of some words, yours to your interlocutors or theirs to you; if so, do not interrupt. In any case, though important, these are not the occasions when you can expect a decision to be reached, so whatever was missed will pop up again. Avoid exaggerating claims. There is a local proverb, "When you hear there are cherries aplenty, bring a small basket."

There is no call to raise your voice, get emotional, or show upset. Cypriots themselves do not do it because of their sense of honor. Women in the room are treated equally, so a silent woman is not an indictment of male attitudes but indicative of her place as a person in the hierarchy along with everyone else.

You may start discussions informally, over coffee, which is a good gesture. In negotiations be professional and persistent. Cypriots generally are direct, but if you feel the other person is obviously trying it on, you don't have to take this lying down and can challenge it. At such an informal level, if they bark, you bark back. If you are still interested, improve your argument, not your shouting. Cypriots are practical people who love a deal. If they respond to a suggestion you make with a series of objections and defer discussion of it to a future meeting, it means you have time to address those objections with better research. If they respond to it negatively with a point of principle, the odds are against it.

Seniority is the gateway to decision-making. The underlings in the room can offer suggestions, but it is not your place to negotiate with them. Address yourself to the person in charge, or his deputy if appropriate, and remember that discussions can be lengthy. Keep negotiations human and civil. It is fine to have someone with you taking notes. Cypriots know how to negotiate skillfully.

CONTRACTS

Usually contracts will be followed to the letter. EU membership means that Cypriot law was harmonized with the *acquis communautaire.* However, the Cyprus legal system is an amalgam of civil law and common law retained by Cyprus after independence from Britain. According to a Cyprus law expert, "The parties to a contract are free to choose the law to govern the whole or part of their contract, even where the chosen law has no connection, or no apparent connection, with the transaction in issue."

A verbal agreement is important but there are so many possibilities for misunderstanding that the sooner it is put on paper the better. If things go awry before the signing and money has already been spent, one can bring in lawyers, but the law is slow moving. As the Cypriot media often remind the country, justice delayed is justice denied. Foreign investors want to know that the legal system will back them, so when some people can influence the outcome of a case with a phone call, it is not encouraging, unless that phone call is for you.

RESOLVING DISAGREEMENTS

Should a dispute arise, arbitration is better than litigation (and has deeper roots), at least for smaller-scale disagreements, because it approaches the two parties on a personal, not an institutional, level. However, having a respected go-between is better than arbitration. The traditional way to resolve interpersonal disagreements was to go to the *mukhtar*, the village leader or elder, who, among other duties, was responsible for administering local justice and maintaining law and order. Today, he or she can be someone who commands respect—a priest, the president of an association you belong to, or an older person of standing. Someone who can intercede quietly and then, if things remain unresolved, simply pull back.

There is also a *méson*, as when a friend might ask you, do you have *méson*? It literally means, the middle, the go-between. At its best, it is to have people next to you who can stand up for you. It is up to you how you handle it or how you act as a *méson* if asked to be one.

Whatever you do, try not to make your business disagreement personal, because then you are offending a wider circle of people who might be related to, or acquaintances of, the person you are having the stand-off with.

TEAMS AND TEAMWORK

Teamwork is an Anglo-Saxon term, and that is where it stays. Teamwork has all the bearings of a "flat hierarchy," and in Cyprus there is no such beast. Hierarchy is vertical all the way to the top, and that is where the final decision is taken. Small businesses remain small by choice because they are their own boss. This is an aspect of Cypriot

For businessmen suits and ties are *de rigueur* in all weathers.

individualism, the feeling that "no one will take decisions for me." In both situations, hierarchy and "own-boss," there is no collective decision-making.

Another perceived drawback of teamwork is having to put the interests of the team above one's own quality of life. It is almost a native instinct for some to try and disrupt teamwork so as not to be overtaken by it. Cypriots are used to defending themselves against foreigners, against a superior, and against each other. And when you do need something, then, as of old, you activate specific connections, rather than a team that is here today, gone tomorrow.

You will find that non-hierarchical, teamwork-oriented Cypriots tend to be on the soft left and are involved in intercommunal initiatives between North and South, not in business. They are people who are comfortable working with diversity, where hierarchies and individualism act as barriers.

BUSINESS ENTERTAINMENT

Entertainment is an extension of business and invariably involves food on the table, such as going out for a meal at a nice location. In Cyprus you are only an hour away from beautiful places. Sometimes you go to a nightclub with your partners, where there is drinking and dancing. Family invitations are not uncommon; the positive feelings that are generated from being good business partners are not restricted to office hours. Hearty eaters are not frowned upon.

GIFTS

What is appropriate and what inappropriate? It is fine to give small gifts. For a first-time meeting when you sit officially to discuss business, a bag printed with the logo of your company containing brochures and a sample of its products, or a small complimentary gift such as chocolates or pens, are fine. If you already know the person and are meeting after having flown in from abroad, you can bring them a bottle of something you know they like, or a box of candies. Some businesses exchange presents at the end of the calendar year. Also acceptable is presenting a gift to your host when invited to a social occasion. Gifts are not opened in front of you.

CONDUCTING BUSINESS IN NORTHERN CYPRUS

There are few regular, accountable assessments of Northern Cyprus' economic performance.

Between Mersin 10 and Northern Cyprus
Due to the international embargo of the TRNC, there are no direct air or sea links with the rest of

the world. Consequently, imports and exports need
to go through Turkey by putting in to the southern
Turkish port of Mersin or via a Turkish airport
where Turkish officials issue certificates if necessary.
As such, the postal and administrative classification
for Northern Cyprus is "Mersin 10." Inquiries to
companies, departments, or officials in the North
are addressed "via Mersin, Turkey."

The reliance on Turkey is pervasive, with
local banks and telecoms able to function only
by integrating with Turkish companies. A good
percentage of Ankara's financial assistance to the
North actually benefits the daily requirements of
thousands of Turks settled there. Further sums
return to the mainland for the purchase of goods,
machinery, and construction materials.

Since there cannot be a viable TRNC currency,
the working currency in the North is the
fluctuating Turkish lira, thereby precluding the
ability to determine an independent monetary
policy. The economy is unable to sustain its public
infrastructure, and civil engineering is wanting.
However, exports of citrus fruit, dairy products,
vegetables, minerals, and scrap are in demand and
remain healthy.

The pandemic interrupted a period of impressive
growth that had deprioritized traditional Western
tourism. Casinos and gambling are illegal in Turkey,
transforming Northern Cyprus into its Las Vegas—
to the discontent of Turkish Cypriots and expats.
At the other end of the tourist market, the North

began catering to a conservative, "Halal-friendly" tourism, observing certain tenets of Islam such as separate beaches for the sexes and a no-alcohol policy. Again, this is a mainland Turkish initiative, at variance with local sensitivities.

Interestingly, there is a very ancient and business-oriented local Cypriot-Muslim institution. The Turkish-Cypriot Waqf is a Muslim charitable foundation established on the island by the Ottomans in 1571, which today owns part of the ROC's Cyprus Airways. It has a large property portfolio throughout the island, created through donations and bequests.

Business Mentality

Foreigners and even Turkish Cypriots in the diaspora consider there is no identifiable business structure to the place, as they understand it. A foreign-born Turkish-Cypriot designer who moved to Northern Cyprus observed, "It feels like a no-man's land because they believe no one is watching." Clearly there are laws and social order, but, he said, "the law here is not a strict procedure."

Though a political minority pushes for partition, the fact that many Turks benefit hugely from the unregulated status of the North indicates that Ankara would prefer it to be a Turkish Hong Kong.

Business Climate and Meetings

There are no short meetings—they can last one, two, or five hours. They usually end when the boss wraps it up. The managing director makes sure everyone is fed and contented. Personal relationships trump colleague relationships. Some people can have such good personal skills that it distracts from fact that they don't have the required competence, and they may go high up the ladder.

Western investors in tourism need to build strong relationships with hoteliers in order to ensure that customers receive the service they expect. Social media has also become important for constructive feedback and an improved service.

The use of credit cards in the North is fine, especially if you have a banking app that messages you immediately that your transaction has gone through. But make sure you know the exchange rate of the Turkish lira to your own currency.

Property and title deeds are the hottest potato on the island. In a landmark case (Apostolides v. Orams) in 2009, the European Court of Justice backed the right of a Greek Cypriot to reclaim his land in the North, which had been sold without his agreement to a UK couple. The safest properties to buy are those owned pre-1974 by Turkish Cypriots or expats, and those Greek and Maronite properties sold by their owners post-1974.

WOMEN IN BUSINESS

In both communities women tend not to discuss money unless they are running a business, especially in the South. Cypriot women have always been strongly represented in the workforce in agriculture and as seamstresses, and have embraced the modern skills required in today's world. At work, they might occupy important but not decision-making positions, in areas such as PR, marketing, advertising, and fashion. However, these positions are providing many with financial independence through their work. The new generation of Cypriot women are gradually gaining partnership positions in law firms and managerial positions in many walks of life. They are strongly represented in the media. Despite the progress made in their status, their individual achievements are not flagged in the same way as men's. At the end of the day, women are still responsible for running the household, and for this reason some would argue that, in many respects and despite the inequalities, Cyprus is a matriarchal society.

CORRUPTION

Cyprus draws attention when it accommodates the ill-gotten wealth of foreign magnates and politicians. On a local level, corruption is often accepted because there is no consistent prosecution against it, and a few politicians are able to use parliamentary immunity to get away with it.

International organizations and the European Commission have criticized corruption and collusion on the island. The Cyprus government tries to be open to the recommendations of respected bodies on how to cleanse its Augean Stables. A policy document by Cypriot experts, including Professor Sir Christopher Pissarides, noted that relatively small societies such as that of Cyprus are prone to problems with transparency and accountability, and the favoring of relatives and professional associates in the process of governance. It highlights that there are "conflicts of interest arising as a result of failing to segregate those judged from those judging." The experts concluded by recommending that the whole "building" be demolished and restructured, but in parliament legislative progress is tortuous.

On Transparency International's Corruption Perception Index (TICPI), in 2020 Cyprus ranked 42nd out of 180 countries, a reasonably fair position. For foreign investors, the independent judiciary system overall ensures the protection of property and contractual rights, and they do not face the challenges that local residents face.

An independent report conducted in Northern Cyprus in 2019, using the TICPI methodology, ranks it a middling 82nd out of 180 countries. It identifies that "the government overall is unsuccessful in the fight against corruption" due to "a lack of good governance." The main areas of concern are bribes, abuse of public resources by ministers and officials, and the near absence of deterrent penalties.

CHAPTER NINE

COMMUNICATING

LANGUAGES AND LOCAL DIALECTS

The official languages of the Republic of Cyprus are Standard Modern Greek (SMG) and Standard Turkish. Greek dominates in the South, Turkish in the North. English is the language of business and is widely spoken in the South, where it can be a challenge to practice your Greek if you are learning it. That said, having at least a survival knowledge of the official languages shows a greater commitment to the country, even if you only use a word or two occasionally. Other languages on the increase are French, German, and Russian.

As mentioned, there is a characteristic Cypriot accent common to all Cypriots, irrespective of their mother tongue. Furthermore, many Greek Cypriots speak in blends of SMG and Cypriot Greek but are disinclined to see it gain official status. What Cyprus has retained and Greece has ironed out is spoken varieties of the same Greek language that shift from one context to another. The official language in national education, the courts, the media, and for official purposes is Standard Modern Greek. A similar linguistic pattern applies to Turkish and the Turkish Cypriots.

In everyday communication between Cypriots, there is a linguistic distinction between town and country. In towns—where the dialect was considered a little "hillbilly"—SMG has always dominated with the occasional use of dialect words and idioms and some minor inflections rooted in Ancient Greek. There is no Standard Cypriot Greek since it varies across the island and there is reluctance to see its rich variations codified. In the North, a similar approach applies to Cypriot Turkish.

Certain wordless sounds mean specific things in Cyprus. The "tut" sound (done by snapping the tip of the tongue against the back of the upper two front teeth), accompanied by the raising of the eyebrows, means "no." If that sound is repeated two or three times, it means "out of the question." Repeated several times in succession while slowly shaking the head means "what a pity," "what a shame," or expresses disapproval, as in "you shouldn't have done that."

DIGITAL PROTOCOLS

The moment Skype calls were available, Cypriots were onto it and there was no going back. The sudden necessity for daily video conferencing imposed by the Covid-19 pandemic raised some interesting cultural questions. There was a brief debate as to whether people could smoke when online. At home a person can smoke without affecting others. A consensus emerged that if you are the boss, no one will say anything; if not, just pop out of sight and have that puff. The more informal the meeting, or if involving people of the same business "*paréa*," the more likely it is for smoking to take place since 36 percent of Cypriot adults smoke. Or if a meeting involves the chairperson who might be a heavy smoker, he might say, it's OK to smoke, but if he smokes and says nothing, no one else lights up.

Do you greet a friend online if you haven't seen them for a while when there are more than ten people at a meeting? In the physical world, face-to-face protocol requires that you acknowledge them verbally, so when online do you break rank, give your greeting, and go back on mute? In some ways it depends on whose patch you are on, who is the host; digital protocols are changing. One thing remains constant: you do not chew gum.

Ultimately nothing will dislodge the centrality of Cypriot café society and face-to-face meetings.

BODY LANGUAGE

Compared to the conventional distance for social interaction and conversations in some Western countries, personal space in Cyprus is closer but with a "British-style" reserve when it comes to physical contact. Handshakes linger a little longer; one person can take hold of the arm of another. This does not happen between men and women, where the handshake is looser and shorter. Air or contact kissing on the cheeks is normal between women and close friends of the opposite sex.

Body language reinforces the intended message. The Covid pandemic may have changed the pattern of physical contact, but gestures are not affected by it. Cypriots are not overly animated. Greek Cypriots are slightly more demonstrative than their Turkish-Cypriot compatriots, more spirited when they talk. Their gestures usually express something specific.

Body language can differ between the groups. This can be observed in the way people stand while socializing in the street in different parts of Cyprus. A small group of Anatolian Turks might form an almost hermetic circle and display minimal movement and gestures, their voices low, their heads slightly inclined as they glance almost cautiously over their shoulders. A Turkish-Cypriot group will form a looser circle; their gestures and shoulder movements will be contained and directed to each other. A Greek-Cypriot group will maintain a loose circle; they will be more visibly interested in the goings-on in the street and, when looking, may partly turn the body as if they are about to leave. You will probably hear a mainland Greek group before you see it.

GESTURES

- Swiping the palms of your two hands together means "That's it, done."
- If you have had enough food or drink and are offered more, it is polite to place the palm of your right hand against your chest, pulling it away and saying, "No thank you".
- Making small vertical circles with the palm of your hand indicates that the person mentioned is exaggerating.
- Older generations will tug or air-tug the top of their garment or tug their collar to indicate that they don't like something, or to communicate "Keep away from him/her," in which case it can be accompanied by saying, "Heaven forbid."
- Rubbing the side of both index fingers together is a suggestion or a question whether two people mentioned are having an affair.
- Spreading out your arms while slightly pulling back your chest and smiling indicates "I haven't seen you for a long time. Good to see you again!" The same, but with a hint of exasperation, means "You are late, where were you?'" or "What have you done?"
- Lifting your open hand higher than your head, not directly above it, palm facing away from your interlocutor and waving it means "That's long gone," or "Forget about it."

Women of all communities are not often observed standing in a public space for social purposes; they seem happier strolling in a line, chatting, perhaps shepherding young children. The personal distance between younger Greek-Cypriot women will fluctuate like an accordion playing a dance tune, while that of Turkish or Levantine women will remain more constant. You will make your own observations and reach your own conclusions.

THE MEDIA

Freedom of speech is guaranteed in the 1963 Constitution. Cyprus has a broadcasting media that wears its partisanship on its sleeve. The Greek-language Cyprus Broadcasting Corporation (CyBC), or RIK, is state funded by the Republic of Cyprus. Its radio and TV channels have news slots in Turkish and English. Some favorite soaps are in the Cypriot-Greek dialect. Mainland Greek channels are streamed in. Radio is very popular, with more than 75 percent tuning into it. There are many independent, often net-based, broadcasters.

Newspapers and magazines are often linked to political parties. *Haravgi* is left, and its coverage is probably the least affected by government sensitivities. *Symerini* is right. *Phileleftheros* is independent center. *Machi* is very nationalistic.

Politis features many debates and is independent. The English-language newspaper *Cyprus Mail* goes back to 1945; it is very informative, with an anti-union tendency. The *Financial Mirror* is a weekly English-language newspaper and comes in a shade of salmon pink; it covers far more than financial news. The 1960 Constitution guarantees freedom of speech and expression and journalists have the right to protect their sources. There is occasionally government intervention, though in general the Cypriot media are careful about exposing people.

The morning ritual of reading the newspapers in a Nicosia café.

The Republic of Cyprus has a lively and polished selection of specialist business information publications that cover all sectors of the economy. They usually provide profiles and contributions by ministers, CEOs, and senior managers.

In Northern Cyprus, freedom of speech is generally respected, but attacks on journalists have become more common. The mainland Turkish government puts pressure on local journalists to refrain from critical reports on Ankara. Bayrak is the main broadcaster, though most people in the North are tuned in to mainland Turkish TV. Northern Cyprus dailies include *Avrupa* and *Yeni Düzen*, which are left-wing and pro unification of the island. *Kıbrıs* has the highest circulation, and *Kıbrıs Postası* probably has the largest online readership. Turkey and the Turkish military have a high level of influence on the Northern Cyprus media, though it is not a "puppet media." *Cyprus Today* is a biweekly with a multinational staff and is the leading English-language newspaper in Northern Cyprus.

Most Cypriot newspapers are available online.

THE ONLINE COUNTRY

Wi-Fi Internet is readily available across the island, in private and public places. Cypriots do like their online connectivity. Around 83 percent of Cypriots aged sixteen to seventy-four have active social media accounts, ranking the Republic of Cyprus

third-highest in the EU. The percentage is higher
among young people. The number of mobile
connections is probably more than 100 percent of
the total population since many have more than
one connected device. Most people use the Android
mobile operating system. Bills can be paid online
through the Cyprus government portal, and almost
all banks offer full Internet banking services, where
transactions can be made online if you have an
account.

Access
The government of the Republic of Cyprus has
achieved 100 percent coverage of the country with
broadband infrastructure, with minimum speeds of
at least 2Mbs and using DSL broadband network.

The percentage of individuals using the Internet
to interact with public authorities, to obtain
information, and to download and fill in official
forms, is lower than the EU average. However,
the percentage increased following the need for
greater online usage brought about by the Covid-
19 pandemic. The government has launched an
educational program to minimize digital illiteracy
and further promote the use of eGovernment
services. The pandemic has enhanced online
education.

A note about roaming fees! Avoid being
inadvertently charged. If your contract allows
you to roam at no additional cost, it will probably
include Cyprus, and may even include Northern

Cyprus. Northern Cyprus does not have its own telecommunications system. It relies on that of Turkey, which is not an EU member state.

The phones or laptops of some people in the South who move close to the border may automatically switch to a Turkish provider. They will then be charged the corresponding Turkish fee, which can be quite steep. Some providers and local SIM contracts treat Cyprus as a single entity. If in doubt, check your roaming clause and prevent your phone from switching providers.

Overall connectivity is good across the island, with glitches at more isolated locations.

The e-Generation

Parents find it difficult to control their children's high usage of social media. It is not so much about the dangers posed, but the waste of time, lack of reading, and the distraction it creates, even among adults. Most young people are on Instagram.

A recurring cause for chagrin across the island is how phones and the Internet are eroding the tried-and-tested traditional ways of life, namely visiting people and talking. However, the young regularly keep in touch with their parents through social media. A Turkish-Cypriot author mused that, in general, life online takes an important chunk out of people's time. He compared daily life today to decades ago when the children of Cyprus had direct contact with nature in all its forms; they would make their own toys, and the playtime songs that children sang spoke of daily rural activities. He concluded that the colorful mosaic of island life was being defeated by technology and apps.

MAIL

Cyprus Postal Services is a state-owned monopoly, which has modern services and is efficient. It is one of the largest companies in the country. There are yellow mail boxes in some streets for letters. There is a tracking system for parcels.

In the North, the region is classified under the mainland Turkish province of Mersin. Mail must be addressed to the receiver by street and town, but

Yellow-painted colonial-era pillar box still in use.

then followed by "Mersin 10, Turkey," because the TRNC is not recognized by the Universal Postal Union.

CONCLUSION

Cyprus has come a long way over the last decades. This book has set out to provide you with insights into what makes the Cypriot people what they are today, and to make you aware of the proverbial paddling that goes on beneath the calm surface. No one expects foreigners to be experts, just to be themselves and, *sigá-sigá*, as time goes by, to feel at home.

Some things have only been hinted at in the book because its remit is not to be exhaustive for its own sake; for instance, the role of UN resolutions, or the cultural magnets that are Athens and Istanbul. And there is the hope of many Greek and Turkish Cypriots for their leaderships to officially exchange that soothing word, "sorry." Not least, and brace yourself for it, there is the wicked Cypriot sense of humor unfolding as your companions cheerfully work their way through a succession of ten, twenty, or more delicious *mezé* dishes, washed down by excellent light Cypriot wine or *raki*.

We hope this practical guide will enable you to develop your own relationships with the people of this beguiling island. So, *kopiáste, hosgeldiniz*— welcome to Cyprus!

APPENDIX: USEFUL APPS

Most of the following apps are free with the usual clauses. The list is not an endorsement of any particular app, but an overview of what is available. Some apps do not allow you to report issues or wrong deliveries, and some can only be downloaded once on the island. Some continue to transmit your location even when switched off and therefore draw on your battery life.

Transportation and Travel

The taxi **CABCY** app connects passengers to a licensed taxi driver and you can order a taxi immediately or for a later time and receive a confirmation. The app was started by a foreigner in Cyprus who saw the need for passengers to be sure they get a good car.

bolt.eu for taxis in both South and North.

2GIS Cyprus provides bus or car routes.

For bus services, the Web site is **intercity-buses.com**. An app can be found on publictransport.com, which allows bus users to plan their journey and gives real time information about their arrival at bus stations.

EnterCy promises to help you personalize your journey.

Places to Stay

visitcyprus.com, the official Cyprus Tourist Office Web site, is not an app but a comprehensive, easy-to-use guide to accommodation with lots of additional information.

TripAdvisor is a standard travel platform for online hotel reservations and booking transportation.

Food

The app **Foody Cyprus** is for online deliveries if you wish to have your dishes brought to where you are.

The app **deliveryman Cyprus** is another one.

bolt.eu covers food as well.

wolt.eu is for food and presents and grocery deliveries.

For food deliveries in Northern Cyprus there is **yemeksepeti kktc**, which means "food basket." It is for Turkey but it includes "kktc" or "TRNC" as part of the Turkish locations it covers.

TripAdvisor offers restaurant reviews, though in a "foody" country such as Cyprus personal recommendations work best.

Entertainment

Chooseyourcyprus is a pan-Cyprus offline digital guide with a more local flavor.

visitcyprus.com is also handy for forthcoming events.

Bazaraki.com, meaning "small bazar," provides free classified adverts in Cyprus. A general comment is that it is up to you whether you trust to give your details.

There are apps for easy-going relationships but those are used during the tourist season by visitors and those wishing to meet visitors.

FURTHER READING

Adil, A., Kernal, B., Mehmet Ali, A., Petrides, M. *Nicosia beyond Barriers, Voices from a Divided City*. London: Saqi, 2019.

Bindloss J., Lee, J., Quintero, J., *Cyprus*. London, Lonely Planet, 2018.

Bryant, Rebecca. *Life Stories: Turkish Cypriot Community, Displacement in Cyprus*. Nicosia: Prior, 2012

Charalambous, G., Christophorou, Ch. (eds.). *Party–Society Relations in the Republic of Cyprus*. Milton Park: Routledge, 2016.

Davey, Eileen. *Northern Cyprus, A Traveller's Guide*. London, New York: I. B. Tauris,1994.

Der Parthog, Gwynneth. *Byzantine and Medieval Cyprus: A Guide to the Monuments*. London: Interworld Publications, 1994.

Englezakis, Benedict; Ioannou, Silouan; Ioannou, Misael. *Studies on the History of the Church in Cyprus, 4th–20th Centuries*. Aldershot: Variorum, 1995.

Goetz, Rolph. *Cyprus – South & North – 50 walks*. Munich: Rother Walking Guide, 2015.

Hen, Francis (Brigadier). *A Business of Some Heat*. Barnsley: Pen and Sword, 2004.

Hunt, David (ed.). *Footprints in Cyprus*. London: Trigraph, 1982.

Kyriacou, Chrysovalantis. *The Byzantine War Hero: Cypriot Folk Songs as History and Myth*. Lanham: Lexington Books, 2020.

Loizos, Peter. *The Heart Grown Bitter – A Chronicle of Cypriot War Refugees*. Cambridge: CUP, 1981.

Loukas, Christina. *Cyprus Cuisine: Middle Eastern and Mediterranean*. Vancouver: Whitecap Books, 2021.

Mallinson, William. *Cyprus: A Modern History*. London: I. B. Tauris, 2005.

Richardson, Colin; Porter, Richard. *Birds of Cyprus*. London: Helm Field Guides, 2020.

Shafak, Elif. *The Island of Missing Trees*. London: Viking/Penguin Random House, 2021.

Varnava, Andrekos. *British Imperialism in Cyprus, 1878–1915: the Inconsequential Possession*. Manchester: Manchester University Press, 2009.

ACKNOWLEDGMENTS

Many people, especially from all the Cypriot communities, have graciously shared their knowledge or contributed comments. In particular I would like to thank: Andrea Bayada; John Caponi; Geoffrey Chesler; Costas C. Costa; the Cyprus Tourism Organisation; Goris and Mary Grigoriades, Archim. Benedict Ioannou; Hasan Karlitas; Klearchos Kyriakides; the A.G. Leventis Foundation; Yasar Halim; Antonella Mantovani; Aydin Mehmet-Ali; Kevin Mehmet of the British Library; Fiona Mullen; the North Cyprus Tourism Centre; Chrysovalantis Papadamou; Chris Parry-Davies; Pierre Petrou; Stanka Stoyanova; Despina Varakla; Mary Yamaki; and Ferhat Yesilada. Any errors are the author's alone.

PICTURE CREDITS

Cover image: *The ruins of Bellapais Abbey in the Kyrenia mountains.* © Shutterstock by MarinaDa.

The photographs on pages 129 and 157 are reproduced by permission of the author.

The image on page 126 is reproduced by permission of Whitecap Books, Vancouver, Canada.

Shutterstock: pages 14, 16, 28, 67, 88, 104, 131, 137, 151 by kirill_makarov; 19, 140 by Nejdet Duzen; 20 by Kirill Skorobogatko; 21 (top) by Petr Pohudka; 21 (bottom) by senai aksoy; 23, 115 by ruzanna; 42 by GaryKillian; 64 by jean.cuomo; 66 by Gardens by Design; 69 by Thanasis F; 71 by Roman Evgenev; 74 by Neil Bussey; 79 by Antigoni Goni; 80 by berdimm; 84 by Utku Demirsoy; 96 by Ioannis Karagiorgis; 100 by Chaykoi; 105 by leoks; 107 by Markos Loizou; 113 by Gus Mclee; 116 by Iordanis; 121 by rontav; 122 (left) by aliasemma; 122 (right) by E Dewi Ambarwati; 134 by vangelis evangelou; 137 by Shemyakina Tatiana; 145, 180 by Olga Donchuk; 148 by Fanis Photography; 150 by FOTOGRIN; 152 by bodrumsurf; 160 by Stas Knop; 172, 187 by Tanya Kalian; 191 by Smoking Lens; 193 by Anna Fedorova_it.

Unsplash: page 142 by Karoly Karkusz.

Creative Commons Attribution-Share Alike 4.0 International license: page 17 © Ensind.

Free Art License: page 102 by A. Savin, WikiCommons.

INDEX